The Secret of Sacrificial Self-Service

Discovering the Spiritual Incentives of Christian Hedonism

T. Dougherty

SLEDGE PRESS

Sledge Press
Cuyahoga Falls, OH

© 2021 Sledge Press

First edition

ISBN-10 0-9908008-2-2 (Paperback)
ISBN-13 978-0-9908008-2-8 (Paperback)
ISBN-10 0-9908008-3-0 (ebook)
ISBN-13 978-0-9908008-3-5 (ebook)

Scripture taken from the NEW AMERICAN STANDARD BIBLE®, Copyright © 1960, 1962, 1963, 1968, 1971, 1972, 1973, 1975, 1977, 1995 by The Lockman Foundation. Used by permission. www.Lockman.org

www.sledgepress.com

To my joyful Christian mother.

God takes pleasure in the pleasure of his people.

~A.W. Tozer

CONTENTS

FOREWORD

Self-interest is a gift from God. Without it, salvation would be impossible. From one end of the Bible to the other, God encourages our whole-hearted search for pleasure and satisfaction.

To some Christians, such a theme may sound misguided, perhaps even worldly. The Bible's strong emphasis on self-denial is often thought to rule out the possibility of such shameless self-affirmation. Self-interest is quickly dismissed as simply one more unfortunate consequence of man's fall from grace, a sort of cancer of the soul. The term "self-interest" is suspected to merely be a more polite way of saying "selfish."

Many other Christians, I suspect, will approach the subject with openness, but also with a measure of reservation. Is this to be another one of those books that makes much of a select few passages in the Bible and silently overlooks a host of inconvenient ones? What sorts of qualifications will be made and what sorts of safeguards established? Is the glory of man to completely overshadow the glory of God before we have made it even halfway through?

As Christians, we are to test everything against the Bible (cf. 1 Thessalonians 5:21, 1 John 4:1), so I cannot blame anyone who would suspend judgment until such time as the evidence (or lack of evidence) seems to merit a verdict in one direction or the other. In fact, I consider this approach commendable. We must all seek out some middle way between being gullible and being completely unresponsive.

A few short words about stylistic choices in this text may prove helpful to the reader here at the outset. Biblical citations are from the New American Standard translation unless otherwise noted. Despite the publication of several more recent word-for-word translations, the NASB is still generally considered the most literal English translation available. It is both readable and trustworthy. Direct quotations from the Bible are found in quotation marks, followed by the citation, e.g. (John 3:16). Biblical paraphrases are followed immediately by the biblical citation in the same manner (though, of course, not in quotation marks). Biblical illustrations and examples, on the other hand, are generally noted as (cf. John 3:16). This usage should help the reader discern whether I'm directly quoting from the Bible, paraphrasing the Bible, or simply suggesting that a passage may be helpful to the reader in support of a particular point.

I have chosen to use lowercase pronouns for God (as many Bible translations do), as I have personally found it to be less distracting to the eyes. I mean no disrespect to God, of course. Uppercase pronouns for God have been retained in quotations from other authors and biblical citations. I have also chosen to use traditional singular male pronouns (as well as the colloquial "they," "them," "their," etc. used in the singular). I mean no disrespect to women; again, I found this traditional usage less distracting and more in accord with biblical and Christian tradition.

I have opted to use the traditional B.C. and A.D. dating, with the A.D. being omitted, as obvious and unnecessary in most cases. By the abbreviation "i.e." I mean, "that is"; by "e.g.", "for example"; by "cf.", "see, for instance."

Italics throughout the work are mine unless otherwise noted. The NASB's original italics (indicating that a particular word isn't present in the original Hebrew, Aramaic, or Greek text) have been omitted.

Percentages have been used in lieu of page numbers for ebook citations; 50%, for example, indicates that the citation is exactly halfway through the ebook (the version in question [Kindle, Google Books, etc.] is noted in the bibliography). There does not seem to be any uniform standard of ebook citations currently, and this "percent complete" seemed readily available and better than nothing.

A very heartfelt thanks is due to many faithful friends who gave valuable feedback and helped with various stages of editing: Leslie Capela, Joshua Haveman, Ruth Hill, Race MoChridhe, Bria Isaacson, Caleb Brown, MB Hwang, Leann Pracht, Alexander O'Broin, Nathaniel Killick, Shelby York, and Sofia Podvisocka.

Special thanks is also due to Serbian artist and photographer Stojan Mihajlov for a great collaboration on an interesting cover design concept.

SELF-INTEREST UNDER THE SUN

Though a great diversity of opinions prevails on the subject of self-interest, perhaps we can all at least agree on this much to begin with: we don't have to look all that hard to spot self-interest on planet Earth.

Take your average, run-of-the-mill restaurant chain, for example. I went to one just yesterday (for my birthday, no less), and I made the following observations. Someone greeted me at the door with a friendly smile, as if they were quite pleased to see me, and promptly led me to a nearby seat. Someone else, just as friendly, came and asked if I'd like a beverage or some pre-food food in preparation for the real food. This person is called a "server," like an indentured servant, and that's what they did; they served me. They gladly took my order whenever I felt inclined to announce it, and they circled back frequently to ask if they could serve me anything else. They did their very best to satisfy my every desire, no matter how exacting. Watching them run here and there at my bidding made me feel a little bit like a king enthroned in a royal booth. (For my next birthday, I may bring along one of those cardboard crowns from the fast-food place to further magnify this effect).

The food the server brought was definitely better than anything I could have made at home, and there wasn't any reason to leave until I was entirely full and satisfied because they kept bringing me more as long as I asked them to. They didn't nag me about my calorie count or health choices or anything. In fact, I think they would have kept bringing me food until my stomach had burst, if I hadn't eventually told them I was satisfied.

It was quite a remarkable experience, all centered around me, the consumer. A whole team of restaurant staff stood ready to fulfill my every passing fancy, sacrificing their time and energy so I could stuff my face without having to lift a finger (not counting the fingers maneuvering the knife and fork, of course).

On the surface, the whole thing appeared very selfless on the part of the restaurant and very selfish on the part of the consumer. They did all the cooking, all the cleaning, all the hustling and bustling, while I simply sat on my duff and ate. If it had been my first time in a restaurant and it had somehow escaped my attention that I had to *pay* for all this wonderful service, it would probably seem as if the whole thing was a sham after someone broke the unpleasant news to me. They all seemed very selfless and self-sacrificing until they went and ruined everything by bringing me a bill.

I imagine I'd replay the whole event over again in my mind with a scowl on my face and a fresh and enlightened pair of eyes. The greeter wasn't really that happy to see me; they had to put on that smile or else they'd swiftly be demoted to bus boy. It's unlikely the server enjoyed my company as much as it seemed; they were merely trying to butter me up for a little something extra at the end. The restaurant wasn't in it for my satisfaction, per se, but rather had in view the prospect of making a profit. If they could make the same profit without having to deal with me at all, they'd most assuredly do it that way instead. I was simply a means to an end; it wasn't my satisfaction, but my wallet that was the real object in view.

It wasn't just one or two of the restaurant staff who wanted something out of it either; down to the very last soul, they were all in it for themselves. The proof of this is easy enough to discover. If I took money out of the equation early on by telling each of them, one by one, that I had no intention of paying them for their efforts, it's highly unlikely they would have kept at it for very long. The failed experiment would strongly suggest that, beneath their smiley, self-sacrificial disguises, they're all selfish little capitalists at heart.

With more consideration, however, I'd probably come to conclude it's really quite a reasonable arrangement. No one forced me to come inside after all. No one pressured me into buying anything. No one held a gun to my head and forced me to eat those last few bites of cheesecake (after I had already been forced to secretly unbutton my pants). I was free to come and go as I pleased. I went because I had a hankerin' for that perfectly-cooked, medium-well ribeye, and had no interest at all in raising a cow or having to skin and butcher old Bessie. I've got stuff to do. I don't like doing dishes and ain't nobody got time for chef school.

If I'm being honest, I went for myself—to fulfill my own desires. It also seems fairly plain that the restaurant employees went for themselves too. With all this unbridled self-interest in the air, you'd almost expect to discover bitterness and fighting among the workers and patrons, yet, in reality, the whole night went off without a hitch. We all parted ways quite pleasantly. Someone said, "Come again soon!" in a cheery voice as I waddled out the door, and, after everything is said and done, I almost certainly will.

As far as I can see, self-interest drives everything I do. Why is it I brush my teeth in the morning and do what I can to make myself presentable? Is it not because I'm concerned with myself and with what others will think of me? Why is it I'm careful when driving to work in the morning? Is it not because I don't want to see myself harmed or inconvenienced by a car accident? Why is it I go to work in the first place? Is it not to have money to satisfy my needs and desires? Why is it my belly hangs over my belt a bit, if not because food is a delight to me and I like to push delight to its farthest reaches? Why is it I watch movies, play games, listen to music, take vacations, or invite guests over, if not because I want to see myself entertained and delighted? Why is it I got married, if not to avoid loneliness and to promote stability, happiness, and pleasure for myself? Why is it I pray, if not because I recognize my need and want to see my need fulfilled by the one who is able to answer?

A natural sense of self-regard seems basic to man. It seems to come standard. As far as I can recall, no one ever had to sit me down to convince me that I should prefer pleasure to pain, happiness to sadness, winning to losing, or being praised rather than being shamed. I always like to see myself satisfied, and never really cared much for personal discontent.

We all seem to assume that others likewise have a high degree of self-regard. A salesman, for example, does everything he can to present the snake oil he's peddling as something that will greatly enrich our lives, apart from which all of life may seem like a lamentable scraping-by. A salesman whose only pitch is that buying his product would be really beneficial for *him* wouldn't be nearly as compelling. A salesman who fails to make any sort of appeal to our self-interest would seem quite absurd.

Adam Smith (1723-1790), the Scottish economist, (sometimes called "The Father of Economics,") noted, "It is not from the benevolence of the butcher, the brewer, or the baker, that we expect our dinner, but from their regard to their own interest. We address ourselves, not to their humanity but to their self-love, and never talk to them of our own necessities but of their advantages."[1] We all understand the basic rule of thumb at restaurants, grocery stores, and car dealerships alike: "Give me that which I want, and you shall have this which you want."[2]

Why is it we form corporations, clubs, or even communities if not because we perceive our own good in it? We increase our own prosperity, security, and comfort by joining hands with others; most of us get to avoid being the unfortunate soul who has to skin and butcher ol' Bessie.

---

[1] Adam Smith, *Wealth of Nations*, quoted in Rogers, Anthology, 157.
[2] Ibid, 157.

It's not just humans either. The world of nature is equally preoccupied with self. Plants stretch for the sun and expand luxuriously as far as they are able, without ever an "After you!" to their fellows. Every plant is hard-wired to seek its own success at any cost. Likewise, most animals form colonies, encourage teamwork, and hunt in packs not out of an abstract sense of duty to one another, but rather because they exponentially increase their own chance of success; each member of the group eats better than it would off on its own.

From this vantage point, self-interest seems so entirely ordinary that we generally don't take time to notice it. It seems something like the nose on your own face. Even though it's always there, it's too close to see without some facial contortions and gymnastics.

In fact, self-interest is so entirely mundane, it would be difficult to imagine a person who didn't have any. A man who was completely disinterested in his own well-being would seemingly struggle to find personal motivations to eat, drink, or even get out of bed. He probably wouldn't make it very far in the world.

I suppose we could imagine a selfless man who has no regard at all for himself, but who loves and cares about someone else, and so keeps himself healthy only to be the caretaker of this other person. Yet, here too, we would be forced to assume some measure of self-interest and self-love, because to love someone is to say that *you yourself* personally value and enjoy them. As C.S. Lewis (1898-1963), the popular British author, noted, "Love, by definition, seeks to enjoy its object."[3] Whether it be a love for pizza, a pet, or another person, love always *loves* what it loves and takes pleasure in the object of its love. The great North African pastor, Augustine of Hippo (354-430 A.D.), likewise said, "Nothing can be the object of love which does not afford delight."[4] To love someone is to delight in another, and to delight in another, you have to be the sort of

---

[3] Lewis, Pain, 639.
[4] Augustine, Semon 159, quoted in O'Donovan, Problem, 29.

person who enjoys being delighted. The 20th century Russian-American philosopher, Ayn Rand, went as far as to say, "a 'selfless', 'disinterested' love is a contradiction in terms: it means that one is indifferent to that which one values."[5]

A person who was truly selfless, in an absolute sense, would be entirely indifferent to everything, a person without any loves or delights or preferences at all. If I wasn't at all concerned about myself or with seeking my own good, it wouldn't make one shred of difference to me whether I was a Christian or not, or whether I ultimately ended up in heaven or not. As it stands now, however, reclining with Jesus in perpetual bliss sounds substantially better than the alternative.

The reality is that I care very deeply about what happens to me, and there doesn't seem to be a way (certainly not any obvious way at least) to turn off this natural sense of concern for myself. It feels a little silly to say it—like some sort of hippie self-affirmation exercise—but, the truth is, I love myself. I don't want to starve to death. I don't want to be publicly humiliated. I don't want to be fired from my job. I don't want to be someone else's slave. These are all very ordinary desires, of course, and at the root of each of them lies a very fundamental sense of self-interest. I have an unshakeable desire to see myself succeed.

Though very few actions under the sun could really be explained apart from the assumption of self-interest, the concept nevertheless seems to evoke a great deal of suspicion. Among Christians and non-Christians alike, the rejection of self-interest is promoted as among the highest of ethical ideals. "It's not about you" is a common Sunday morning sermon theme heard across the planet each week (not to mention the title of several popular Christian books). We're often encouraged to stop factoring *ourselves* into our decision-making process, and we're commonly left with the impression that we should learn to live with total self-disregard, without ever a thought of personal gain. I admit, it sounds pretty

---

[5] Rand, Virtue, 44.

good. It definitely has a pious, sacrificial ring to it. And while there may very well be elements of truth in that message, I want to suggest there are almost always elements of misunderstanding as well.

Not that you should take my word for it. The Bible says God declares his thoughts to us in his Word (Amos 4:13), and that we only know something truly when we know it as God knows it (cf. Psalm 139:17). In a certain sense, we only think properly when we think God's thoughts *after him*, that is, when we've let the Bible renew our minds and reshape our thinking (cf. Romans 12:2, Ephesians 4:23). The Bible reveals God's way of looking at things, and human wisdom is found in duplicating these ideas and patterns inside our own brains. To honor God, we must reflect God's thinking. As Christians, "we have the mind of Christ" (1 Corinthians 2:16), and, naturally, we become more Christ-like as we think God's thoughts after him with greater clarity and consistency.

Therefore, my intention in these pages is to scour the Bible in search of God's wisdom as to what role self-interest should play in our day-to-day lives as Christians. God is glorified in our sincere search to unearth his thoughts, and we are always blessed by the discoveries we make. As it is written, "It is the glory of God to conceal a matter, but the glory of kings is to search out a matter" (Proverbs 25:2).

TWO SORTS OF TREASURE

The Bible frequently affirms that it's a good thing to want the best for yourself. Listen to what Jesus said about seeking your own good. This passage will serve as the cornerstone of much of what follows, so I will include a bit of the surrounding context:

> Whenever you fast, do not put on a gloomy face as the hypocrites do, for they neglect their appearance so that they will be noticed by men when they are fasting. Truly I say to you, they have their reward in full. But you, when you fast, anoint your head and wash your face so that your fasting will not be noticed by men, but by your Father who is in secret; and your Father who sees what is done in secret will reward you.
>
> Do not store up *for yourselves* treasures on earth, where moth and rust destroy, and where thieves break in and steal. But store up *for yourselves* treasures in heaven, where neither moth nor rust destroys, and where thieves do not break in or steal; for where your treasure is, there your heart will be also.
>
> *(Matthew 6:16-21)*

Jesus doesn't say anything like "It's not about you" in this passage. His message here is not at all "Go on and work for the kingdom of heaven, and don't you dare expect anything in return!" Quite the contrary; he commands us to store up—to hoard!—spiritual treasure for ourselves. Treasure and rewards are good things that we should desire for ourselves, provided they're the right sort of treasures.

Who doesn't love treasure? Treasure is great. I want treasure. Rewards you say? Yes please, I'll have some. Far from discouraging self-interest or personal gain, Jesus encouraged our reward-seeking behavior. He helped us see how heavenly rewards are much more valuable than earthly rewards, so that we will pursue the work of his kingdom joyfully, not begrudgingly (cf. 2 Corinthians 9:6-8).

Let me make the point boldly: it is the very command of our Lord himself to store up treasure and rewards for yourself in heaven, and to deny yourself these rewards (or to deny that you should seek rewards for yourself at all) is both unfaithful and disobedient. It is not optional, but imperative to seek the Father's rewards for yourself. Samuel Bolton (1606-1654), the English clergyman, noted, "As it is a sin to slight the consolations of God (Job 15:11), so it is no less a sin to make light of the encouragements of God."[6]

Oftentimes, we imagine a good deed is *most* moral when we don't personally gain anything from it. Yet, if this were true, then Jesus' teaching to do good deeds, in order to lay up treasures for ourselves in heaven would have to be seen as second-rate moral teaching. Though the notion that the best sorts of deeds don't look forward to any personal rewards is very pervasive, it can be seen—in direct contradiction to Jesus—as, ultimately, a wrong-headed, worldly notion. The contemporary Christian author, Randy Alcorn, rightly noted:

---

[6] Bolton, Bounds, 89%.

> If we maintain that it's wrong to be motivated by rewards, we bring a serious accusation against Christ. ...If rewards are a wrong motive, then he was luring us to do wrong. This is unthinkable. Since God does not tempt his children, it's clear that whatever he lays before us as a motivation is legitimate. It's not wrong for us to be motivated by the prospect of reward. Indeed, something is seriously wrong if we are not motivated by the promise of reward made by our God.[7]

Far from dishonoring God, seeking spiritual rewards is an act of faith that glorifies God by taking him and his promises seriously. If you didn't have faith in God, you wouldn't seek rewards from God, now would you? "He who comes to God must believe that He is and that He is a *rewarder* of those who seek Him" (Hebrews 11:6). It's not a question of God's glory *or* my rewards, rather God's glory and my rewards go hand in hand. The more seriously I take God's promise of rewards, the more seriously I take God *himself*, for God cannot be divorced from his own promises. God is honored and glorified by our sincere search to take full advantage of his promises. To deny his rewards is to deny God the pleasure of demonstrating his love and generosity toward us. Though many well-meaning church leaders suggest that we should shun all thought of personal gain, Jesus very plainly said that we need to get busy stashing away treasure for ourselves, and, friends, God can hardly forbid what he explicitly commands!

Seeking spiritual rewards from God is, in truth, the *only* way to put God and man in their proper perspective, to see God as powerful, rich, and gracious and yourself as weak, poor, and needy. The man who imagines himself to have overcome the need for such trivial incentives from God seemingly imagines himself to be self-motivated and self-sufficient for good works, but what is this but

---

[7] Alcorn, Rewards, 103-104.

pride? It may disguise itself as self-sacrificing humility, but, much like the Pharisee making his face gloomy when fasting, this is only a disguise.

Of course, Jesus doesn't want us to seek any old treasure, but only the very best treasure. The Pharisees fasted in order to be perceived as spiritual by others, but this was exceedingly foolish. They wanted to be seen by men, and, no doubt, they were seen by men, so, seemingly, they got what they hoped to get out of it. Yet this pointed to a very short-term, earthly perspective. They received the reward they sought, but what a poor reward it was.

"You accept glory from one another," Jesus rebuked them, "but do not seek the glory that comes from the only God" (John 5:44). Clearly, their error lay not in the fact that they sought glory for themselves, but rather in the fact that they sought the wrong sort of glory, and in the wrong way. It's all a question of motive. Beneath a thin spiritualizing veneer, they were motivated by a shallow vanity that tended to cut God out of the equation altogether. They pretended to be spiritual, even though, in truth, they were spiritually desolate, unconcerned about God entirely. It goes without saying that God is not glorified where God is not genuinely regarded.

Jesus had a much different perspective. His eyes were fixed on the long-term, invisible, spiritual reality. He did the math for us, and he knew that a billion years of glory is more valuable than a mere moment of earthly vainglory. He knew there are good investments and bad investments, and he commanded us to seek the very best investments for ourselves, the ones that pay the longest and have the best returns. No one in heaven ever regrets investing in heaven, but there are others who must forever regret cashing in on their rewards too soon.

The hypocrite Pharisees traded an eternity of genuine glory in heaven for a moment of shallow glory on earth, and Jesus pointed out that this is short-sighted, irreligious, and really just plain dumb from a healthy, long-term, spiritual perspective. You should not seek the wrong sort of treasure "for yourselves" (v. 19), but, rather, you should seek the right sort of treasure "for yourselves" (v. 20). Clearly then, those people who say we shouldn't seek *any sort* of treasure for ourselves have fallen short of thinking *God's thoughts after him.*

Oftentimes, we are inclined to dismiss every secondary or "ulterior" motive as inherently wrong, but this is not always the case. We have to sift through our various motives one at a time and examine the quality of each of them. If we serve Christ because we love Christ, and, at the same time, because we want a reward from Christ, these are both good, God-honoring motives. We need not spend time worrying about the proper ordering of these two good motives, for the two always work together to encourage and strengthen one another. To perceive Christ's heavenly rewards is to love Christ more, and to love Christ more is to perceive that love as a heavenly reward in itself.

There's nothing wrong with seeking treasure for yourself, yet material treasure is highly perishable. Those who place all their hope in this world's treasure, "whose portion is in this life" (Psalm 17:14), must forever fear the moths, the rust, and the thieves, and be fraught with anxiety over the prospect of losing their earthly, worldly treasure.

The ancient Greek philosopher, Heraclitus (c. 535 - c. 475 B.C.), said, "You never step into the same river twice," since all of the water is displaced from moment to moment, and all of the previous fish have since moved on. The sand, rocks, and silt at the bottom have also all shifted a little since the last time you stepped in, with some being swept away with the current. From a certain microscopic perspective, almost all the features of the river are different each time you step into it. This is not the place to inquire into what exactly Heraclitus was getting at, but we can say, generally, it seems like a fitting description of our world.

Very few things in this world last very long. We live short, rocky lives full of twists, turns, and setbacks. First, there's twenty years of being bullied and battling insecurities while getting ready for the "real world," and then another decade trying to get established in a career and starting a family. And even if you're fortunate enough to lay down some roots, land a good job and a loving spouse, and find some peace and stability in life, you'll certainly notice by that point that your back doesn't feel as good as it used to. You'll find you can't eat all the same junk food you used to without feeling like the walking embodiment of garbage in the morning. You'll see very clearly that death has laid claim on you and isn't all that far away now. Man is of few days, each of which is full of trouble (Job 14:1). Everyone hates something about their life; this transient world is far too unsettled to provide anything beyond a transient peace on its own.

While the Pharisees made it their treasure to be vainly praised by men, that sort of thing is always doomed to be frustrating. No matter who you are or how high you make it up the social ladder, people are going to insult you, talk bad about you behind your back, and disagree with you on important issues. In fact, the more you manage to get into the public eye, the more people will point out your flaws and laugh at your setbacks. It seems like famous people spend a lot of energy trying to avoid the spotlight, just as countless ordinary people spend all their energy trying to get into the spotlight, blissfully unaware of all the dangers ahead.

Ironically enough, vain people with bloated egos are the same people who are most easily unsettled by the criticism of others. Seemingly, the very thing they place their hope in is what causes them the most suffering. The more we fixate on any earthly treasure, the less it seems to satisfy. As C.S. Lewis noted, when we pursue sin, "an ever increasing craving for an ever diminishing pleasure is the formula."[8]

---

[8] Lewis, Screwtape, 210.

It's quite different with those who store up their treasure in heaven, however. Their treasure is just as imperishable as Jesus' promises. They have a permanent treasure, and all the armies in the world working together in perfect unison with peak military precision could never take a single penny from them. The hearts of the spiritually-minded are able to rest at ease in this great joy and satisfaction, knowing they have laid up an everlasting reward from their beloved Savior. Thomas Manton (1620-1677), the English Puritan, said,

> A child of God whose heart is fixed on God, though there be a great change made in his condition, is where he was still. But a wicked man's hope and comfort ebbs and flows with his estate; when his estate is gone, his confidence is gone.[9]

Really, the best way to say it is "where your treasure is, there your heart will be also." To place your treasure in the turbulent stream of this life is to set your heart in a turbulent stream. Seeking a treasure in heaven, on the other hand, is to set your heart peacefully in heaven *despite* the turbulent stream. "He that lives much in the thoughts of heaven, lives much the life of heaven, that is to say, thankfully and cheerfully."[10] To set your eyes upon heaven's treasure is to establish your heart in heaven while still here on earth. Jesus commanded us to make this our regular habit, and what a wonderful commandment it is!

---

[9] Manton, Self-Denial, 42%.
[10] Bolton, Bounds, 91%.

Our Lord constantly emphasized this sharp distinction between good, spiritually-minded investments and bad, worldly investments. After feeding the 5,000, many people flocked to Jesus simply because they liked the free food, but this was again exceedingly short sighted:

> Jesus answered them and said, "Truly, truly, I say to you, you seek Me, not because you saw signs, but because you ate of the loaves and were filled. Do not work for the food which perishes, but for the food which endures to eternal life, which the Son of Man will give to you, for on Him the Father, God, has set His seal." Therefore they said to Him, "What shall we do, so that we may work the works of God?" Jesus answered and said to them, "This is the work of God, that you believe in Him whom He has sent."
>
> *(John 6:26-29)*

Consider it! Though concealed in a sense, the same God who created the cosmos with a mere breath, as if it were a trivial matter, stood right before their eyes. As owner of everything, having all power and knowledge and ability, he could have bestowed on them all the riches of heaven and earth, pleasure and satisfaction beyond all current comprehension in the blink of an eye. And what did they ask for? A hunk of bread! How poorly they understood the invisible reality of the situation! The earthly immediacy of their hungry bellies blinded Jesus' audience from seeing the spiritual reality right in front of their noses. "It was an inestimable mercy that God should send His Son, yet they looked no further than the loaves!"[11]

---

[11] Manton, *Self-Denial*, 77%.

I'm not convinced we're much better off. For example, someone might think to themselves, *Yeah, that's really silly; rather than asking him to miraculously multiply a loaf of bread, they should have brought him a bit of gold or some coins or gems to multiply indefinitely.* Here too, they'd still be thinking too small. Do the math; what's more valuable, gold that lasts a billion years or gold that lasts only fifty? Jesus could have given them gold beyond measure right then and there, and he could do it for us today, in an instant, if he saw any benefit in it. But when this life, from God's everlasting perspective, lasts only a moment, like a single breath (Psalm 144:4) or the morning dew which quickly evaporates (James 4:14), how valuable really is this world's gold? All this world's wealth is no better than a chunk of bread from that perspective, for they're both consumed in a mere moment.

Jesus himself placed little emphasis on acquiring possessions. He was effectively homeless after leaving Nazareth at the beginning of his ministry. He usually crashed at Peter's house in Capernaum (cf. Matthew 8:14, Mark 1:29); he didn't bother with so much as a pillow for his head (Luke 9:58). The world's wealth clearly meant very little to him.

The Son of God had known trillions upon trillions of years of satisfaction and riches in heaven alongside his Father, and to offer us only the momentary trifles of the world's wealth would have been infinitely less loving of him. It would have been far too narrow-minded for a man with an infinite mind. This world's wealth is not so much wealth as it is a potential distraction from wealth from an eternal perspective.

Jesus showed us how God would think and act if God were a man, because Jesus was the perfect and harmonious union of God and man. He taught us to not fixate on the visible, fleeting treasures of this world, but rather to focus on that which lasts for all eternity. Though it is completely invisible, a sincere faith in Christ is "more precious than gold which is perishable" (1 Peter 1:7).

Two Sorts of Sacrifice

The Bible undoubtedly places a tremendous emphasis on self-denial and personal sacrifice. We will look at a number of those passages at some length in chapter eight. For the moment, however, I would simply point out that since Jesus is the Son of God, we know Jesus' view of self-denial must ultimately be consistent with his command to lay up treasures for ourselves in heaven. How are we to make sense of this?

Here I would suggest Jesus has already laid much of the groundwork for us: there is one sort of treasure to deny yourself and yet another sort of treasure you are to pursue. While we are commanded to be self-denying when it comes to certain worldly treasures, we are nevertheless simultaneously called to be self-affirming when it comes to storing up imperishable heavenly treasures for ourselves. This simple little distinction will go a long way in helping us to understand biblical self-denial.

As Christians, we are certainly called to make sacrifices. Notice, however, when Jesus calls us to sacrifice this or that earthly treasure (such as seeking the vain praise of others), he doesn't ask us to do it merely in the name of self-sacrifice, as some mystical end in itself, but rather for the sake of a better, longer-lasting treasure. We sacrifice perishable goods to gain imperishable goods.

Jim Elliot (1927-1956), the modern American missionary, became determined to bring the good news of forgiveness through Jesus Christ to an unreached group of tribesmen in Ecuador. These tribesmen were in such spiritual darkness, they didn't even have a word for "god" in their language. Local people called them the "Aucas," that is, the "Savages," since they would sometimes murder people outside of their tribe apparently for sport or entertainment. Elliot was very much aware of the dangers, having lived nearby for several years, but persisted in his mission of mercy and love.

Shortly before his death at the hands of the people he was trying to help, he wrote in his journal, "He is no fool who gives what he cannot keep to gain what he cannot lose."[12] That sums it up perfectly. As Christians, we sacrifice something relatively unimportant to gain something immeasurably important. Christian sacrifice is an investment in my future self, a deferral of treasure and rewards, a laying up of rewards for later, where they last forever and never rust or fade. We walk by faith, taking God's promises seriously, and we sacrifice some aspects of our short little lives on earth to gain a far greater treasure just a moment or two from now, in heaven. I love the way Thomas Brooks (1608-1680), the English Puritan, put it:

> Faith sets the recompense, the reward, before the soul (Hebrews 11:25-26). Oh! Says faith, look here, soul, here is a great reward for a little work; here is great wages for weak and imperfect services; here is an infinite reward for a finite work. Work, yes, work hard, says faith, O believing soul, for your actions in passing pass not away; every good work is as a grain of seed for eternal life."[13]

---

[12] Eliot, Shadow, 108.
[13] Brooks, Heaven, 65%.

Christian sacrifice is a rational spiritual investment. It's never sacrifice for the sake of sacrifice, but rather the joyous sacrifice of a small treasure for a great treasure:

> The kingdom of heaven is like a treasure hidden in the field, which a man found and hid again; and from joy over it he goes and sells all that he has and buys that field. Again, the kingdom of heaven is like a merchant seeking fine pearls, and upon finding one pearl of great value, he went and sold all that he had and bought it.
>
> *(Matthew 13:44-46)*

Christian sacrifice never calls for lament or self-loathing, but rather for celebration. Christian sacrifice is like going to a yard sale and finding a million dollar baseball card hidden in the bottom of a box and then "sacrificing" fifty cents for the box. Listen to the way the Apostle Paul described his rationale for living a life of sacrifice:

> I do all things for the sake of the gospel, so that I may become a fellow partaker of it. Do you not know that those who run in a race all run, but only one receives the prize? Run in such a way that you may win. Everyone who competes in the games exercises self-control in all things. They then do it to receive a perishable wreath, but we an imperishable. Therefore I run in such a way, as not without aim; I box in such a way, as not beating the air; but I discipline my body and make it my slave, so that, after I have preached to others, I myself will not be disqualified.
>
> *(1 Corinthians 9:23-27)*

Paul here envisioned the Christian life as an Olympic race. He imagined God crowning the winner with a laurel wreath, the glory of which would never fade. This race is not against our fellow Christians, but against our sin and our inclination to seek only earthly treasure. Seemingly, Paul had no intention of disregarding himself as far as this race was concerned. Rather, he ran so as to take the first place prize into his own hand. Like an Olympian in training, he disciplined his body to stay in peak spiritual shape. He focused constantly on spiritual conditioning and self-control, so as to direct every ounce of his energy into the end goal of winning the prize. Most Olympians run for a prize that lasts a few years and is soon forgotten, but Paul wanted an eternal prize from the hand of God himself.

Paul was dead serious about God's promises and didn't try to deny himself spiritual rewards. In fact, the whole reason he was willing to sacrifice his earthly goods and comforts—indeed, his very life—was because his eyes were fixed intently on heaven and heaven's treasure. He served others for the sake of the gospel. He became all things to all men (9:22) to win over some of them. He denied himself countless earthly comforts in order to win that invisible, imperishable victory wreath. Looking through the eyes of faith, he saw his sacrifices for others as being, at the same time, investments in himself. He had, after all, forsaken his old life as a Pharisee in favor of a greater treasure. "Whatever things were gain to me," he wrote, "those things I have counted as loss for the sake of Christ" (Phillipians 3:7).

If we were to judge by outward appearances—by a purely visible, worldly standard—he must surely appear to be an epic failure: beaten, bruised, berated, lacking basic necessities, and, ultimately, beheaded. Yet, by his own testimony (in his very last letter), he was playing the long game, he was playing to win, and indeed, he did win:

> ...the time of my departure has come. I have fought
> the good fight, I have finished the course, I have

kept the faith; in the future there is laid up for me the crown of righteousness, which the Lord, the righteous Judge, will *award* to me on that day; and not only to me, but also to all who have loved His appearing.

(2 Timothy 4:6-8)

Many Christian leaders suggest we shouldn't seek awards such as praise, glory, or honor for ourselves, but quite to the contrary, Paul said we *should* "by perseverance in doing good seek for glory and honor and immortality" (Romans 2:7). The Apostle Peter likewise said the result of our faith is "praise and glory and honor" from God and "joy inexpressible and full of glory" (1 Peter 1:7-8) upon Jesus' return. It's good to want glory and honor and praise for yourself, but it has to be sought from the proper source. Very soon God will "disclose the motives of men's hearts; and then each man's praise will come to him from God" (1 Corinthians 4:5).

C.S. Lewis noted that it is imperative to make a clear distinction between sinful pride and a healthy desire to be praised:

> Pleasure in being praised is not Pride. The child who is patted on the back for doing a lesson well, the woman whose beauty is praised by her lover, the saved soul to whom Christ says 'Well done,' are pleased and ought to be. For here the pleasure lies not in what you are but in the fact that you have pleased someone you wanted (and rightly wanted) to please. The trouble begins when you pass from thinking, 'I have pleased him; all is well,' to thinking, 'What a fine person I must be to have done it.'[14]

We could take this a step further. When a toddler wants to please his mother by offering her a crayon stick-figure drawing and is

---

[14] Lewis, *Mere*, 106.

subsequently rewarded with his mother's praise, laughter, and applause, we all understand this is not something sinister, but something beautiful. We can't let the mere existence of sinful, worldly treasures trick us into thinking we shouldn't seek any sort of treasures at all!

We can't let the presence of worldly pride completely overshadow the fact that there is a place for a normal, healthy sort of pride. In fact, there is even a proper place for boasting in the Christian life, namely in the high and lofty standing we have before God in Christ (cf. Galatians 6:4, 1 Corinthians 1:31). This sort of boasting is, curiously enough, a sign of true humility (cf. Psalm 34:2). As a sinner, I have to hang my head in shame, but as a Christian, shocked back into spiritual consciousness by the Holy Spirit and reborn in the image of Christ (cf. Romans 8:29), I have to regard myself highly, even to the point of boasting about how great I am *in him*!

The same sort of distinction applies to seeking glory, praise, honor, and other sorts of spiritual treasures and rewards for ourselves. Worldly men seek one type of praise, honor, and glory while the Christian, walking by faith, seeks an altogether different type. The Christian sacrifices the perishable versions of these treasures to gain the imperishable versions, where the men of this world sacrifice the imperishable to gain the perishable.

In my experience, this sort of talk makes some people very uncomfortable. They feel that praise should flow from man to God and never the other way around. They suspect that if man is praised, God has had that same praise stolen from him.

Think back to the example of the mother praising her child for the stick figure drawing. The child hands over the drawing as a sincere act of affection for his mother, and the mother rightly takes delight in her child's demonstration of love. She can hardly hold back the laughter and applause. In fact, if she were forced to stifle her praise and applause, it would diminish her own joy. The mother's praise for her child is not in any way to her detriment, but rather represents the culmination of her own satisfaction. Her joy is incomplete until she praises her child, for praise is the natural outworking of love.

In the same way, God's praise to us for running well does not in any way detract from God's pleasure or glory, but adds to it. "The Lord takes pleasure in His people" (Psalm 149:4). If God were to stifle or restrain his praise for his beloved, he would simultaneously stifle his own pleasure and glory.

Many people fear they would be "using" God if they sought eternal rewards from God. They know a sinful heart can twist good promises to evil ends, and so they turn their eyes away from the promise, for fear of spoiling it. This is not a real solution, however, for we are called to run hard after God's promises.

Part of the problem here is a failure to clearly distinguish a legitimate search for heavenly treasure from one that is hypocritical. The Pharisees viewed God as a means to the worldly end of prideful vanity. A religious hypocrite demonstrates he has no real interest in God, because the moment the earthly treasure is in hand, God is cast aside. A Christian, on the other hand, recognizes God as the source of every earthly gift and blessing (James 1:17) and he uses his earthly treasures unto the end of his spiritual service. He is even willing (in his better moments at least) to sacrifice his earthly comforts if God calls him into difficult service for some greater spiritual end (such as difficult missionary work), because above all else he seeks the reward of God's affirmation upon his life.

Where a religious hypocrite uses God for earthly treasure, a true Christian uses earthly treasure for God, because the Christian understands that God himself is the greatest of all treasures. "Good men use the world in order to enjoy God, whereas bad men want to use God in order to enjoy the world."[15]

I have a finicky cat who sometimes brushes up against me affectionately when he's hungry. Best as I can tell, however, he has no real affection for me, for he only comes near me or shows me

---

[15] Augustine, City of God, quoted in Nygren, Agape, 506.

any affection when he wants food. That leads me to believe his affection is not sincere, at least not in the fullest sense, because he has no real interest in me, but only in the food I am able to fetch for him. I am nothing more than a means to some other end.

Perhaps I'm judging him and his little cat motives too harshly, but I'm fairly confident that if he were larger than me, and thought he could get the food faster simply by knocking me out of the way like a rag doll, he would definitely do that instead. To him I am nothing but the food gatekeeper, more of an obstacle to manipulate and overcome than anything else. As a result, I find the whole display of him brushing up against me more annoying than endearing. Maybe he could fool another persnickety cat with that nonsense, but I'm wise to his tricks. Now, notice carefully, it would be one thing if he loved both me *and* the food; that would be perfectly fine, perfectly healthy and normal. Sadly, however, my cat only "loves" me on account of the food, and so I consider him a sort of unconscionable, hypocritical feline. And so it is with the world. The hypocrite sacrifices heaven for earth, where a true Christian is willing to sacrifice earth for heaven, for he perceives the enduring value of God's eternal rewards (cf. Matthew 16:26-27).

Seeking treasure from God honors and glorifies God by acknowledging, through faith, that he is the all-sufficient source of treasure. It also glorifies God inasmuch as a faithful person recognizes God's goodness and benevolence in God's generosity and so responds naturally with affection, gratefulness, and thanksgiving to God. If it is "using" God to seek good things from God, then it would be using God to seek heaven or Christian contentment (or even God himself!), but this would clearly entail some very muddled thinking.

A Christian must seek both God and God's eternal rewards. To seek God's rewards without also seeking God *himself* is hypocrisy. To seek God without seeking God's rewards is to dishonor God by refusing to obey his blessed command to lay up treasures in heaven.

Two Sorts of Self-Interest

Now maybe you're asking yourself, *what difference does it make if I get treasure and rewards in heaven? It's not as though there are going to be beggars up there.* That's very true, yet Jesus clearly assumed some folks will be better at laying up treasure in heaven than others and, throughout the Bible, there are countless indications of degrees of rewards for faithful service.[16] Paul said, very plainly, "each will receive his own reward according to his own labor" (1 Corinthians 3:8). How can it be though that everyone in heaven is perfectly happy while having this sort of inequality among them? The answer proposed by the brilliant American Puritan, Jonathan Edwards (1703-1758), seems to me to be entirely satisfying:

> It will be no damp [or diminishment] to the happiness of those who have lower degrees of happiness and glory, that there are others advanced in glory above them. For all shall be perfectly happy, every one shall be perfectly satisfied. Every vessel that is cast into this ocean of happiness is full, though there are some vessels far larger than others. And there shall be no such thing as envy in heaven, but perfect love shall reign through the whole

---

[16] In addition to the passages already quoted, you could look at parables such as Luke 19:11-27, where faithful people are rewarded in accordance to their earthly effort, as well as other explicit teaching passages such as Matthew 13:23, Mark 10:40, 2 Corinthians 9:6, and Revelation 22:12..

society. Those who are not so high in glory as others, will not envy those that are higher, but they will have so great, and strong, and pure love to them, that they will rejoice in their superior happiness. Their love to them will be such that they will rejoice that they are happier than themselves; so that instead of...[diminishing] their own happiness, it will add to it. They will see it to be fit that they that have been most eminent in works of righteousness should be most highly exalted in glory. And they will rejoice in having that done, that is fittest to be done. There will be a perfect harmony in that society; those that are most happy will also be most holy, and all will be both perfectly holy and perfectly happy. But yet there will be different degrees of both holiness and happiness according to the measure of each one's capacity... The exaltation of some in heaven above the rest will be so far from diminishing the perfect happiness and joy of the rest...that they will be the happier for it; such will be the union in their society that they will be partakers of each other's happiness.[17]

Edwards suggested while there is an endless supply of happiness to be had in heaven, some will have a greater capacity to take it all in. Each of us will have our glass filled to the brim with joy and pleasure and satisfaction, but some glasses will be larger than others. To put it in more modern-day American terms, if heaven is an all-you-can-eat buffet of happiness, some folks will always have a greater appetite than others (and, of course, no one will ever get fat!).

If we stop and think about it for a minute, even in this life, each person has differing capacities for knowledge, faith, joy, and so

---

[17] Edwards, Portion, 902.

forth, so it shouldn't really surprise us to discover not everyone in heaven will be identical. The Holy Spirit gives a diversity of gifts on earth (cf. 1 Corinthians 12) and the same trend will undoubtedly continue in heaven. There will still be a beautiful diversity in heaven, with various sorts of gifts allocated to each person in various degrees in accordance with their earthly effort. Far from this being an occasion for complaining, we will personally delight in one another's delight, having had our love perfected, as one big happy family. For the first time ever, we will all be completely and sincerely dedicated to one another's success.

Today we live under the curse of the fall (cf. Genesis 3), and sometimes we get so used to the curse we think of it as normal. We struggle to imagine what life would be like without the weight of sin. Imagine it. When our hearts are perfected, the joy of others will never (ever) be cause for jealousy or envy, but rather cause for celebration. The joy of others will be a joy to us. The Renaissance hedonist and Roman Catholic priest, Lorenzo Valla (1407-1457), concluded on this point, "I dare say that whoever is most beautiful, adorned, and blessed [in heaven] will give the most joy and happiness to all the others. Hence I maintain without doubt that the goods of the individual and of the whole are here identical."[18]

So then, bliss for all is not incompatible with degrees of rewards, but actually complementary to it. A heaven without some contrasting flavors wouldn't be a heaven at all, now would it? "If all experienced God in the same way and returned Him an identical worship, the song of the Church triumphant would have no symphony, it would be like an orchestra in which all the instruments played the same note."[19]

Another question seems to emerge here, however. Given that it will add to my personal contentment in heaven to know that others are more content than I am, why should I be overly concerned about spiritual rewards? It's not as though I'm going to

---

[18] Valla, Pleasure, 297.
[19] Lewis, Pain, 642.

be upset that I have a lesser capacity for pleasure than others. I will actually enjoy the fact that they have a greater capacity than I do.

This is, of course, quite a lazy question, but it's also a very pressing question, for sin has made us quite lazy in the pursuit of spiritual rewards. God holds out "pleasures forevermore" (Psalm 16:11) in both hands, and encourages us to take all we can carry, yet we just can't be bothered with eternal pleasures so long as our Netflix™ accounts are still active.

Here we have to recognize God wants what's best for us even more than we do, for we often define our best interest in worldly terms and on very short timelines. Comfort and leisure are not bad things, yet being overly committed to our own earthly comfort and leisure is the safest and surest way to miss out on a world of opportunity. It requires very little effort to sit and do nothing, yet the Bible wants us to recognize that our lethargy and laziness are contrary both to God's glory and to our best interest. The question, then, is this: if God doesn't want you to settle for second best, why should you be content with second best? God wants you to run so as to win, and you're not ultimately doing yourself any favors by resting content with last place. You'll never regret running hard for the true prize.

Keep in mind, heaven will not be a disembodied, ghostly state, but, rather, a redeemed Earth.[20] We will still have physical bodies, but those bodies will be free from every defect (cf. Romans 8:19). Heaven will be a place of both spiritual and physical pleasure. All of the physical pleasures we enjoy on Earth we will almost certainly enjoy there as well, and new pleasures will be added. Heaven will be pleasure upon pleasure without any defects or distractions. It will be pleasure upon pleasure without any intermingling of stress or anxiety, fear or loss.

Clearly then, heavenly treasure is something you should

---

[20] Randy Alcorn's book *Heaven* does a great job dispelling the notion that heaven will be a disembodied state. Heaven is the New Earth, and the New Earth is simply the Earth redeemed and entirely fixed.

desire for yourself. You should seek to attain the highest capacity for pleasure you can. You should lay up treasures in heaven all the time, and you should never try to restrain yourself from laying up treasure in heaven, for that would be contrary to Jesus' wonderful command.

To me, this comes as a tremendous relief, for it strongly suggests the problem is not self-interest, as such, but simply a misdirected, worldly self-interest. It's not that I have to deny myself every sort of treasure. Rather, I have to rethink what sorts of treasure I should pursue. It's not that I have to rid myself of self-regard. Rather, I have to *redirect* my self-regard to God-honoring goals and ends.

Satan appealed to man's self-interest even before the fall had occurred. He suggested to Eve that the forbidden fruit would increase her knowledge and perhaps even her power and influence (cf. Genesis 3: 5-6). His sales pitch included the promise of personal benefits. It's evident from this that self-interest existed before the entrance of sin in the world. To be sure, self-interest has now come under the sway of sin's influence. God created man morally upright, and man subsequently corrupted himself (Ecclesiastes 7:29). Self-interest as it exists now is corrupt in many ways, but it wasn't that way originally, and it certainly won't be that way in heaven.

Just as there are two different sorts of people in this world pursuing two different sorts of treasures, so too there are two different sorts of self-interest. Just as the Bible distinguishes between a worldly "old man" and a righteous, born-again "new man" (cf. Romans 6:6, Ephesians 4:22-24, Colossians 3:5-10), so too each of these has his own variety of self-interest.

There is, on the one hand, the self-interest of the old man who sets his eyes exclusively on the world's bread, the world's treasure, and the world's praise and reward. This is the sort of self-interest the Bible repeatedly condemns (cf. Proverbs 23:6, Romans 2:8, Philippians 1:17, 2:3, James 3:14-16). This type of worldly self-interest is what would most properly be called "selfishness." The men of this world "seek after their own interests, not those of Christ Jesus" (Philippians 2:21). They pursue their own pleasure with disregard for God and others (cf. 1 Corinthians 10:24). The old man may pay God some lip-service for one earthly reason or another, but ultimately he acts without regard to God as he has revealed himself. Some people, like the Pharisees, "pay a pennyworth of imaginary humility to Him to get out of it a pound's worth of Pride towards their fellow-men."[21] The old man is a short-term thinker who defines his good according to the immediate urges of his belly. His *desire* is evil because he desires what is evil.

There is also a sort of self-interest, however, that sets its eyes on the eternal treasure in light of Christ and biblical truth. We might call this sort of self-interest "redeemed self-interest." While both the old man and the new man seek their own good and their own interests, the new man heeds Jesus' advice about where his best interest actually lies. In faith, the new man learns to trust God and to think God's thoughts after him. He takes God's investment advice about what sort of treasure is really the most valuable. "I advise you," said the glorified Savior, "to buy from Me gold refined by fire so that you may become rich, and white garments so that you may clothe yourself" (Revelation 3:18). It's good to *desire* so long as you desire what is good (cf. Galatians 5:16-23).

There is a worldly self-interest that sets its eyes on the things of the world, as if this life is all there is, but there is also a redeemed self-interest that walks by faith and not by sight, and sets its eyes on the eternal prize. By "redeemed self-interest," then, I mean our natural, God-given sense of self-interest put back in its proper, original place, subordinate to God and God's commandments. Human self-interest is messed up on account of the fall, certainly, but it's not beyond God's ability to reshape, to renew, and, ultimately, to redeem.

Far from rejecting self-love and self-interest,

---

[21] Lewis, Mere, 105.

> The Scriptures, from one end of the Bible to the other, are full of motives that are set forth for the very purpose of working [only] on the principle of self-love. Such are all the promises and threatenings of the Word of God, its calls and invitations, its counsels to seek our own good, and its warnings to beware of misery. These things can have no influence on us in any other way than as they tend to work upon our hopes or fears. For to what purpose would it be to make any promise of happiness, or hold forth any threatening of misery, to him that has no love for the former or dread of the latter?[22]

The Bible constantly warns us to stop looking to sin for satisfaction, but it never asks us to deny our own ultimate, long-term best interest. When the Holy Spirit prompts us to read our Bibles, he is simultaneously prompting us to obtain the personal blessing of reading it. The Bible has countless lessons to teach us about the ways to attain peace, joy, and satisfaction. The Word of God yields countless earthly and heavenly rewards (cf. Psalm 19). The reason we don't read it often enough is because we fail to recognize the immense personal value held out to us.

With an open hand, God holds out rational incentives to rational, self-interested creatures:

> God always deals with men as reasonable creatures, and every word in the Scriptures speaks to us as such. Whether it be in instructing [or] teaching us, he gives us no commands to believe those things which are directly contrary to reason, and in commanding us [to obey him] he desires us to do nothing but what will be for our own advantage, our

---

[22] Edwards, Charity, 160.

own profit and benefit, and frequently uses this argument with us to persuade us to obey his commands.[23]

While we often take Jesus' command to lay up treasure in heaven for ourselves very lightly, sometimes even rejecting it at a practical level, the personal significance held out to us can hardly be overstated. Jesus incentivizes Christian sanctification by commanding us to seek our own long-term good in following him. "Blessed are those who hunger and thirst for righteousness, for they shall be satisfied" (Matthew 5:6). Don't you see it, friend? Jesus was clearly saying it's *good* to want to be satisfied! You should crave, with everything in you, to be satisfied! You shouldn't try to find satisfaction in sin like the world does, however. The place to look, rather, is in righteousness.

The Bible teaches that self-interest can be redeemed, and that a redeemed sense of self-interest can be an extremely powerful tool unto Christian renewal and sanctification. In stark contrast to the world's ethical ideals (as well as the ethical ideals of many Christians), my suggestion is, if you're not in it *for yourself*, then you're doing it all wrong.

---

[23] Edwards, Christian Happiness, http://edwards.yale.edu (Edward's complete works are available for free here).

TWO SORTS OF HEDONISM

In the last few chapters, we began laying the foundation for a biblically re-invented, God-centered vision of self-interest. I join a growing chorus of others in referring to this vision as Christian Hedonism.

Generally, when we think of "hedonism," we imagine people fulfilling all of their earthly pleasures through unrestrained gluttony, orgies, drunkenness, and so on, and to be honest, that's a pretty good description of what hedonism originally was. This is not the place for an in-depth survey of ancient, pagan hedonism, but a few quick highlights may prove helpful, especially in connection with the Bible.

The term "hedonism" comes from a Greek word referring to pleasure, especially sensory, physical pleasure.[24] The earliest self-proclaimed hedonists originated from Cyrene, in Greece, in the 4th century before Christ. They argued it is self-evident that all creatures seek pleasure and avoid pain. For example, if you pick a large rock up off the ground, any bugs which may have been hiding underneath will immediately scatter in order to avoid potential harm to themselves. Similar examples could practically be multiplied indefinitely. Unfortunately, the "Cyrenaics" were also sceptical

---

[24] The Greek ἡδονή (pronounced **hēdonḗ**) is transliterated in English as "hedone." It may be worth noting that, in Greek mythology, Hedone was the daughter of Eros, and the personification (and deification) of pleasure and delight. (The Roman parallel was found in Voluptas ["Pleasure"], daughter of Cupid).

about the prospect of an afterlife. They argued that since each of us will soon cease to exist, we can do no better than to enjoy earth's pleasures. The ancient slogan "Eat, drink, and be merry, for tomorrow we die" seems to have been representative of their general outlook.

As a cultural movement, the Cyrenaic philosophy was short-lived, for the reality never quite seemed to live up to the ideal. At times, their popular motto was mocked and parodied as "Eat, drink, and be merry; for tomorrow we shall have gout, cirrhosis of the liver, and delirium tremens."[25] Cyrenaic hedonism was a practical philosophy of life that wasn't very practical outside of the glory days of youth. It offered a highly perishable sort of pleasure, and tended to leave the middle-aged physically broken and spiritually despondent.

In light of the apparent failure of the Cyrenaic school, a second group of hedonists, founded by a fellow named Epicurus (341-270 B.C.), thought it better to define pleasure negatively, as avoidance of pain, rather than the active accumulation of pleasure. The Epicureans thus emphasized moderation and sometimes even abstinence from certain pleasures, if those pleasures could later result in pain. They went so far as to teach that we should be content with what we have, avoiding envy, love of money, prostitutes, and other vices that can later lead to unintended consequences and unwanted pain. They often defined the "good life" as simply the quiet life of learning.

Like the Cyrenaics, the Epicureans taught that there is no afterlife and that earthly pleasure is man's highest aim. As Epicurus put it, "We call pleasure the alpha and omega of a happy life."[26] Epicureanism had a very long life span. In fact, several hundred years after Epicurus' death, the Apostle Paul spoke to a group of Epicureans in Athens on his second missionary journey (cf. Acts

---

[25] Cf. Clark, Thales, 151. *Delirium tremens* is delirium or confusion caused by withdrawal from alcohol.
[26] Epicurus, Essential, 33%.

17:18), around 50 A.D. It didn't go very well, for they "sneered" at him for his teaching about the resurrection of the dead (17:32 NIV), though a few were converted (17:34).

The same skepticism concerning the resurrection of the dead later reappeared in the church in Corinth (cf. 1 Corinthians 15). Corinth, it should be remembered, is a Greek city only about sixty miles west of Athens. In response to this skepticism, Paul argued that if it is not possible for God to raise the dead, then even Christ himself could not have been raised from the dead, in which case our Christian hope is in vain (15:13-14). Faith in a dead Christ is a worthless faith (15:17). A belief in the resurrection is, therefore, fundamental to Christian faith. Like Christ in his resurrection, so too we will trade a perishable body for an imperishable body (15:53). Paul rebuked the Corinthians for keeping bad company (15:33), presumably with Epicureans, and admonished them to never rest content with the world's fleeting treasures in light of Christ's promises. He concluded, "Therefore, my beloved brethren, be steadfast, immovable, always abounding in the work of the Lord, knowing that your toil is not in vain in the Lord" (15:58).

There is certainly no shortage of the "eat, drink, and be merry" mentality in our world today, and the Bible seems to view this as the default outlook of the worldly-minded in every age (cf. Ecclesiastes 2:24, 8:15, Isaiah 22:13, Luke 12:19). It makes sense upon its own assumption, of course. If this life is all there is, investing in heaven is childish nonsense. The crucial difference between the pagan and the Christian is, of course, *Christian faith*. Ultimately, it is a question of whether or not Jesus is trustworthy. If he was telling the truth about there being an enduring afterlife following our few short years here, then it makes much more sense to live for that life rather than just for this one.

Notice, the real point of dispute between Paul and the ancient hedonists was not *if* we should pursue what's best for us, but rather *where* we should pursue it. Unbelief says we should pursue our best interest only on earth, where faith says we should pursue our best interest in heaven. Paul even went so far as to concede the point that if there is no afterlife, this life is obviously as good as it gets. "If the dead are not raised," he said, "let us eat and drink, for tomorrow we die" (1 Corinthians 15:32).

Likewise, while Jesus recognized two different types of treasure-seekers, he didn't acknowledge a third group of non-treasure-seekers. All men pursue either this or that treasure. Jesus never bothered to ask whether or not we all want treasure for ourselves, for it's obvious that we all do. All men desire the best for themselves and all men are, in that sense, hedonists. Again, the question was never whether or not we should seek pleasure, but *where* we should seek it.

Both the ancient hedonist and the Christian Hedonist agree that you *should* pursue your own pleasure to the fullest extent possible. They disagree, however, as to where to find lasting pleasure. Whereas the ancient hedonists all seemed to disagree as to the best way to achieve lasting pleasure, the Christian Hedonist presents the question to God himself as he reads his Bible. One important discovery he makes early on is that the perishable pleasures of earth pale in comparison to heaven's enduring pleasures. In short, if ancient hedonism is living for pleasure, defined in a very worldly way, Christian Hedonism is living for pleasure from the big-picture, God-honoring perspective of the Bible.

While some folks will inevitably find the term "hedonism" scandalous and offensive, I would submit for their consideration that the Apostle Paul (obviously no stranger to ancient hedonism) used the Greek term "hedonista"[27] twice in his next letter to the Corinthians.[28] Paul was obviously aware of the worldly connotations this word had acquired over the past few centuries. Written to an often wayward church congregation located in the

---

[27] ἥδιστα (pronounced hā'-dē-stä) is transliterated in English as "hedista" or "hedonista." It means "with great pleasure."
[28] 2 Corinthians 12:9 and again in verse 15.

very heart of Greece, there's zero chance those connotations would have been lost on his audience. Clearly, Paul wanted to raise eyebrows. I suspect he wanted to cause a little scandal in the hearts of his readers. He wanted to draw the hearts of a worldly congregation away from the fleeting pleasures of this life and toward the true, lasting pleasures—the hedonistic pleasures!—of a godly life. I hope I can do the same in the pages that remain.

Being thoroughly committed to laying up treasure in heaven and getting your heart into heaven while still on earth is what I mean by "Christian Hedonism." It is not, in any way, a less moral (or morally loose) deviation of Christianity, but rather the vigorous reaffirmation that it's a good thing to want what's best for yourself, provided you heed God's advice about what really is best for you. God genuinely and sincerely wants what's best for you and he wants it for you on a permanent basis. He also wants *you* to want what's best for you on a permanent basis. That's why he commands you to seek treasure in heaven rather than on earth. You should seek pleasure all the time, but you should seek it where it can actually be found.

Heaven on Earth

It may be a helpful bit of context about your author to know that I work in retirement planning. The company I work for helps other companies set up and run their corporate retirement plans; that's how I make my living. I've been at it for over thirteen years now.

The main idea behind a retirement plan in the United States is pretty simple. You put some money into a plan on a tax-deferred basis. "Tax-deferred" means you don't pay taxes now, but you do pay taxes when you take the money out in the future, generally when you're no longer working, which is to say, after you retire. The system works reasonably well, because every party involved gains something meaningful for themselves.

The employer sets up a plan because it helps with employee retention, saves on corporate taxes and payroll taxes, and costs them almost nothing. The employee puts money into the plan because it saves on their personal taxes immediately and allows them to save for the future and to try to secure a future retirement for themselves. Uncle Sam does it because it's a fairly inexpensive way to ease the burden on the government to provide a safety net for older citizens. In most cases, the government also takes a cut of the investment earnings when you take the money out, so in a way, the government is playing the stock market along with the retirement plan participant all those working years.

There may be one or two points of comparison with Christian Hedonism, of course. To this point, I have primarily argued that Christian sacrifice is an investment in the future. It's not entirely unlike a retirement plan. Instead of taking all your money and spending it on soda pop and bubblegum as an early reward to yourself, you defer some into your 401(k) plan, as an act of love toward your future self. It's a "deferral" in the sense that you're not simply throwing it away or discarding it, but rather delaying its receipt until later. It's a temporary sacrifice for your own ultimate good. You give up a little treasure now to gain a lot more treasure later. The idea of stockpiling a little something for the future is a very simple idea anyone can appreciate, whether in terms of earthly or spiritual investments.

When it comes to spiritual investments, however, a subtle mistake sometimes creeps into our thinking at this point. This mistake is what I want to focus on in this chapter. It's a very subtle error, so you'll have to pay close attention or else you might miss it. Here it is, plain as day: oftentimes, we imagine the Christian life to be a forgoing or deferring of earthly life in order to gain heavenly life. In other words, we imagine the Christian life as a sacrifice of the current life for the sake of the next life. In other words still, we imagine we must sacrifice current, earthly pleasure to gain a later, heavenly pleasure.

Did you miss it? It sounded a lot like what I've been saying all along, didn't it? It really has a nice ring to it, and even though it's dead wrong, to many Christians it will sound more or less correct. There was a subtle change in my wording, and sometimes this change slithers in so subtly we don't notice it at all. While it's certainly true that we have to forgo the life of *sin* and the life of *sinful pleasures*, it's totally and completely wrong to imagine we have to forgo life *itself* or the life *of pleasure*. To many folks, this may sound counterintuitive, if not downright contradictory, but bear with me a few moments.

As we have said, the old man seeks his reward sooner rather than later. He is a short-term hedonist rather than a long-term hedonist. He imagines the best way to find satisfaction is to seek it right now, as soon as possible. He wants the praise now, the money now, the sex now, and so forth. He doesn't think too much about the future, so he's willing to take whatever moral shortcuts are necessary to get right to the action. It's a smash-and-grab, immediate, direct approach to satisfaction. The old man doesn't think much about sacrificing to others, because he's very focused on his own immediate gain. He's not an investor but a consumer. He assumes that seeking pleasure immediately, regardless of pesky moral commands, is the safest and surest path to pleasure, and because he loves himself and his own pleasure, that's exactly what he does.

The reality, however, is that sin doesn't bring sustainable pleasure. The ventures of the worldly tend always toward failure and frustration. Money is an easy example. The fear of the loss of money, the obsessive concern for getting more money, and the jealousy and envy over other people's money all converge to sap all the real pleasure right out of it. Money is viewed outside of its proper perspective, and thus from a faulty and foolhardy perspective, and this ends up ruining everything good about it. "The love of money is a root of all sorts of evil, and some by longing for it have wandered away from the faith and pierced themselves with many griefs" (1 Timothy 6:10).

Money is a good thing, but sin has a tendency to ruin it for us. When used in a worldly way and viewed from a worldly perspective, money becomes a point of worry and frustration, taking on elements of competition and contention with others. We become slaves to our money, as if the money were behind the scenes, running the whole show. Take a look at some of the troubles caused by this sort of worldly ambition:

> Now the deeds of the flesh are evident, which are: immorality, impurity, sensuality, idolatry, sorcery,

enmities, strife, jealousy, outbursts of anger, disputes, dissensions, factions, envying, drunkenness, carousing, and things like these, of which I forewarn you, just as I have forewarned you, that those who practice such things will not inherit the kingdom of God.

(Galatians 5:19-21)

In the context of money, we can see right away that a worldly love of money potentially involves almost every item on this list (which, Paul indicated, is by no means comprehensive). Love of money can obviously lead to enmity, strife, jealousy, anger, disputes, dissension, envying, and so on. Do any of these things bring pleasure to us? Not at all; all of these things bring suffering to our doorstep. The deeds of the flesh all have in common that they are a burden to us; they suck the pleasure out of everything. The deeds of the flesh are all self-defeating, self-destructive deeds.

There is, of course, something absurd about the miser who refuses to spend or enjoy the money he has; his wealth has seemingly become worse than useless to him, for it serves no purpose outside of stressing him out. "There is a grievous evil which I have seen under the sun: riches being hoarded by their owner to his hurt" (Ecclesiastes 5:13). The miser lives under the sway of sin's delusion. He imagines that he is winning in life even as his wealth drives him farther and farther into misery, isolation, and spiritual poverty.

We have also seen the same tendency in human vanity. "Pride is spiritual cancer: it eats up the very possibility of love, or contentment, or even common sense."[29] The vain person has a bloated and over-sensitive ego that makes them intolerant of criticism or correction. Men shove their way into the spotlight, but find only a world of misery there, when they could have travelled a better way. They set themselves high upon the pedestal of their own

---

[29] Lewis, *Mere*, 106.

heart, only to find themselves constantly knocked down by the fact that others fail to take notice of their transcendent significance. They are envious of the successes of others, but consider:

> It is the most foolish kind of self-injury; for the envious make themselves trouble most needlessly, being uncomfortable only because of others' prosperity, when that prosperity does not injure themselves, or diminish their enjoyments and blessings. But they are not willing to enjoy what they have, because others are enjoying also.[30]

Now I'm not denying that sin can be fun and exciting. No pleasure-seeking sinner (like me) could take such a view seriously. Nor am I denying that sin can, on some occasions, provide a short-term advantage. Lying can, no doubt, sometimes save us a lecture or some personal embarrassment. Stealing can certainly be a quick shortcut to financial gain. I'm not denying that. I'm simply saying any pattern of sin always brings unwanted baggage with it, and the baggage always ends up outweighing the pleasure on anything but the shortest of timelines.

Nobody trusts a liar or a thief. Everyone has to guard against them, weapons drawn. If you look closely, you'll see that every aspect of their lives is negatively affected by their sin. Their sin brings them some short-term benefits here and there, of course, but those benefits come at a tremendous cost in terms of unintended consequences. Their sin affects who they are, how they deal with others, and how others deal with them, not to mention the spiritual and eternal ripples and repercussions.

Like a drug, sin distracts you with a little pleasure and a few dividends up front, while at the same time sneaking a world of suffering in the back door. (Drugs themselves can be loads of fun, no doubt, but if you visit the local meeting of Narcotics

---

[30] Edwards, Charity, 127.

Anonymous and listen to the stories of the bleary-eyed folks who would give everything they had to escape their slavery, you'll certainly conclude it's not a desirable path to travel down). And that's how all sin is.

To cite one further example, looking at pornography might not seem like the end of the world, but (very cautiously), do an internet search for "porn induced erectile dysfunction" and you'll learn very quickly that millions of men have literally traded away real sex for mere pictures. They didn't consent to it, of course; it's just that pornography started calling the shots at some point along the way. As a teenager, you might think of porn as a sex-substitute you'll only need until you have the real thing. It's just a little shortcut, a little life hack. In time though, you learn that despite all your best intentions to the contrary, pre-marriage pornography ended up taking a massive toll on your married sex life.

Porn trains a man to seek a shallow, instant gratification. A real woman, on the other hand, requires romance, reassurance, and communication. When a man who has known nothing but instant gratification encounters a situation requiring genuine effort and delayed gratification, he'll find it frustrating, and he'll simply take the easier route. The young Christian may have planned to quit as soon as the ring went on his finger, but that turned out to be sin's deception. He'll discover himself to be the same person the day after he got married that he was the day before he got married, and he'll follow the path sin has trained him to take all along.

A man who is overstimulated by porn is almost certain to feel under-stimulated by the reality of a real woman (generally beset with a host of insecurities) in a real bedroom. Satan always wants to push us as far out into the darkness as he can, and the more a person lets down their guard and lets themselves be led down that wide road, the more over-the-top and immoral their tastes in pornography will become, and the less exciting real sex will appear (hence the ever-increasing prospect of erectile dysfunction).

Now it pretty much goes without saying that the pleasure of pornography is not worthy of comparison with the pleasure in the marriage bedroom between two people who have known true intimacy and genuinely want to satisfy one another. Only an imbecile would trade real money for a photo of money, and, likewise, only an imbecile would trade real sex for a mere picture, but that's exactly what happens. Though envisioned as a short-cut to satisfaction, or perhaps even an accessory to satisfaction, the ugly reality is that true satisfaction is traded for shallow satisfaction, and the more we become enslaved to it, the more the shallow satisfaction comes to resemble isolation and all-out despair. There's an ever-increasing craving but an ever-diminishing pleasure.

To put it as plainly as possible, a pornography addiction inevitably leads to a worse sex life and to less real sex in the long run. As a form of covetousness, it makes you restless and discontent with what God has given you. To lust is to wage war against your own soul (1 Peter 2:11). The man who thinks he can outsmart the system and be the exception to the rule is deluding himself.

In all these examples, you can see that taking the moral shortcut and seeking your reward too soon leads to diminished returns not just in the future, but also right now—in this life here today. Do you suppose the Pharisees were satisfied by their vanity? They received the reward of their own bloated self-estimation, of course, but at what cost?

The suffering caused by sin always outweighs the pleasure gained through sin. This is the Bible's uniform testimony. "Bread obtained by falsehood is sweet to a man, but afterward his mouth will be filled with gravel" (Proverbs 20:17). Sin is always its own punishment. "In the mouth of the foolish is a rod for his back" (Proverbs 14:3). Sin is always a sin against yourself, that is, a sin against your own well-being. "They lie in wait for their own blood; they ambush their own lives" (Proverbs 1:18). Sin never gives any lasting satisfaction, and never confers any lasting benefits. "What benefit," asked Paul, "did you reap at that time from the things you are now ashamed of?" (Romans 6:21). We always suffer injury on account of our wrongdoing (2 Peter 2:13). We are always weighed down by our own iniquities (Isaiah 1:4). "Many are the sorrows of the wicked, but he who trusts in the Lord, lovingkindness shall surround him" (Psalm 32:10).

Foolish as they were in many regards, even many of the ancient pagan hedonists were smart enough to know that a pleasure should be avoided if it would bring suffering in its wake. Epicurus' advice is sound for the most part:

> Since pleasure is our first and native good, for that reason we do not choose every pleasure whatever, but often pass over many pleasures when a greater annoyance ensues from them. And often we consider pains superior to pleasures when submission to the pains for a long time brings us as a consequence a greater pleasure. While therefore all pleasure because it is naturally akin to us is good, not all pleasure is worthy of choice, just as all pain is an evil and yet not all pain is to be shunned. It is, however, by measuring one against another, and by looking at the conveniences and inconveniences, that all these matters must be judged.[31]

Sadly, Epicurus was stuck in a short-term mindset without any personal hope of heaven. A Christian Hedonist, on the other hand, has the advantage of relying upon God's long-term perspective when measuring one pleasure against another. He studies his Bible and concludes that sin never works for very long. All sin has the tendency to ruin pleasure and personal satisfaction while at the same time trying to trick us into believing that sin is the surest way to get ahead.

---

[31] Epicurus, Essential, 34%.

We never truly *enjoy* sin in the fullest sense of the word, for the pleasures of sin are always riddled with guilt, unrest, self-loathing, and embarrassment. "'There is no peace,' says my God, 'for the wicked'" (Isaiah 57:21). The old man imagines that taking the path of moral shortcuts is the quickest way to arrive at the destination of persistent peace and pleasure, but always ultimately discovers that the shortcut is actually a dead-end.

Moral shortcuts and the shallow pleasures of sin always end up detracting from the substantial, God-given pleasures in life. The more we do any activity in a sinful way, the more it will enslave us and the less we will enjoy it. Sin is never a good investment—not now and not later. Don't take my word for it though; I'm just some guy who works in retirement plans. The Bible itself promises that the Christian life holds all the promises for this present life:

> Discipline yourself for the purpose of godliness; for
> bodily discipline is only of little profit, but godliness
> is profitable for all things, since it holds promise *for
> the present life* and also for the life to come.
>
> *(1 Timothy 4:7-8)*

Physical exercise gives a little profit in healthy moderation, but it can hardly be compared to consistent spiritual exercise. The exercise of godliness is immensely profitable, and it's not just a deferral of pleasure until you get to heaven (as if to suggest that sin is where all the real earthly pleasure is). Rather, righteousness is profitable both in "the present life" and the next, for in giving up the shallow satisfaction of sin you'll find true satisfaction in doing things the way God originally intended.

Here's what I mean: working hard for things will be more consistently satisfying than stealing. Sex within marriage will be more consistently satisfying than sex in any other context. Seeking peace with people will be more consistently satisfying than lashing out at them when you get irritated. Being honest with people will be more consistently satisfying than lying to people. Being content with what you have will be more consistently satisfying than being jealous of others. Being a Christian will be more consistently satisfying than being anything else, and so on and so forth. God is the author and inventor of every earthly pleasure, and he considered everything, covered all the angles, and didn't overlook a thing.

God did not make man for sin, but for righteousness, and if you think sin works better than righteousness in practice, you're mistaken. God's commandments are not oppressive or burdensome (1 John 5:3), but rather represent liberation from sin's blinding and unhappy enslavement. Listen to the way Moses himself summarized God's commandments:

> "Now, Israel, what does the Lord your God require from you, but to fear the Lord your God, to walk in all His ways and love Him, and to serve the Lord your God with all your heart and with all your soul, and to keep the Lord's commandments and His statutes which I am commanding you today *for your good?*
>
> *(Deuteronomy 10:12-13)*

When I was younger, I thought it was a little crazy for the Psalmist to cry out "O how I love your Law!" (119:97), for I imagined the law to be oppressive in some regards, as stifling man's true satisfaction in sin, but now I see that this was sin's delusion at work in my mind. The sin that was killing me had tricked me into believing it was best for me. My sin caused me to misdiagnose my true predicament. I guzzled down sin's poison and thought myself clever for it.

Thinking God's thoughts after him implies sharing God's interests with him (cf. Matthew 16:23). Thinking his thoughts implies following in his footsteps. We must follow after his heart (1 Samuel 13:14) and walk in his ways (Deuteronomy 28:9). "You shall therefore be holy, for I am holy" (Leviticus 11:45). God's commandments are good for you, for the commandments represent doing things the way he would do them. Doing what God would do if he were in your shoes is the best way to do anything. If there were a better, more profitable, more pleasurable way to do it, certainly God would do that instead, since he knows everything.

When we sin, we deem ourselves to be smarter than God, as if we know a secret shortcut to pleasure that he doesn't. We act as though God could learn a trick or two about attaining satisfaction by following our lead. Yet this is the world's great folly. "When we want to be something other than the thing God wants us to be, we must be wanting what, in fact, will not make us happy."[32] In commanding you to obey him, God is expressing his love toward you and his desire for your persistent happiness and pleasure.

The basic principle underlying every last one of God's commandments is that we shouldn't seek pleasure where pleasure cannot be found, and we should seek pleasure where pleasure can be found. Counterintuitive though it may seem to a sinner like me, God's commandments are the true pathway to hedonistic pleasure. Through the commandments, God establishes a clear boundary marker between "life and prosperity, and death and adversity" (Deuteronomy 30:15). If you want the best out of life, pick up your Bible and do what it tells you, because God designed the whole system and there aren't any moral life hacks that actually work.

All sin brings suffering. "Every vice is by its nature hateful."[33] Those beset by the self-inflicted wounds of sin must flee to the Great Physician, whose prescriptions always work best when used as directed. Do you really believe that Jesus is out to detract from your pleasure and happiness on earth when he tells you to obey him? If that's what you think, you haven't yet fully grasped

---

32 Lewis, Pain, 577.
33 Valla, Pleasure, 277.

that "the order of the divine mind, embodied in the divine law, is beautiful."[34]

To love God's law is to love your own life. God's hatred of sin and God's love of righteousness are sewn into the very fabric of creation (cf. Romans 1). All of nature is irrevocably set on rewarding righteousness and punishing sin. We all love to see the wicked get what's coming to them. We all pitch in here and there to ensure that justice is served to liars and thieves. That's just how it is, for a righteous God created this world.

Though the passage is often neglected and misinterpreted, Jesus was very clear that the Christian life is the best possible life on earth:

> And He said to them, "Truly I say to you, there is no one who has left house or wife or brothers or parents or children, for the sake of the kingdom of God, who will not receive many times as much *at this time* and in the age to come, eternal life."
>
> *(Luke 18:29-30)*

Matthew's version of the same teaching has some subtle differences. The two shed more light on one another, and complement one another quite beautifully:

> Everyone who has left houses or brothers or sisters or father or mother or children or lands, for my name's sake, will receive a hundredfold and will inherit eternal life. But many who are first will be last, and the last first.
>
> *(Matthew 19:29-30)*

According to Luke, Jesus said that for every sacrifice we make for the kingdom we'll receive "many times" as much in heaven.

---

[34] Lewis, Psalms, 37%. I removed Lewis' capitalization of several words here, as it seemed somewhat random.

Matthew is a little more specific: "many times" is a "hundredfold." Furthermore, Luke notes that the gain applies not just to heaven, but both "at this time and in the age to come." Putting these side by side, you can readily see that Jesus promised that the Christian life is a one hundred-fold gain on *both* sides of the grave. The Christian life of earthly sacrifice is, ironically enough, a one-hundred fold gain in terms of the quality of earthly life. Even though a sacrifice, by definition, must cost you something (cf. 1 Chronicles 21:24), the curious thing about Christian sacrifice is that it comes at a greater personal benefit.

Now, Jesus obviously didn't mean we need to forsake our "house or wife or brothers or parents or children" in an unqualified sense, but only in a qualified sense. The meaning is not that we have to automatically kick our children out on the streets when we become Christians, but rather we have to love God incomparably more than all earthly relationships (cf. Deuteronomy 13:6-10). Being a Christian entails acting like a Christian, and this will always be disruptive to our old patterns and relationships. Our spouses may leave us, our kids might hate us, our parents might disown us, but we must nevertheless press on in the faith, seeking the imperishable wreath from our heavenly Father. When mom and dad abandon you, God will take you in (Psalm 27:10).

Becoming a Christian always entails a measure of suffering and alienation from the world but, ultimately, this makes Jesus' hundred-fold promise that much more striking. Despite whatever is lost when we forsake our sin, God has promised us we'll still end up with a hundred-fold gain in this life. As Edwards put it, God will "not be your debtor, but will requite you a hundred-fold *even in this life*, besides the eternal rewards that he will bestow upon you hereafter."[35] And again:

> If you place your happiness in God, in glorifying
> him, and in serving him by doing good, —in this

---

[35] Edwards, Charity, 183.

way, above all others, will you promote your wealth, and honour, and pleasure *here below*, and obtain hereafter a crown of unfading glory, and pleasures forevermore at God's right hand.[36]

Sometimes I tell myself *if only I had invested in Google or Amazon or Apple or Microsoft or Bitcoin (or, heck, even Yahoo, AOL, or MySpace) at the right time when I was younger,* but those investments are nothing compared to the ones Jesus spoke of and, so long as you're still here reading this, there is still time enough to invest! If only we were as fixated on spiritual investments as we are on earthly ones, our hearts would be so full of joy and thanksgiving and of everything that matters, and not just in heaven, for our hearts would be in heaven even right here today. There is no risk and no fear of loss when you invest in Christ:

> If those we have full confidence in desire to borrow anything of us, and promise to pay us again, and to pay us a hundred-fold, we are not afraid to venture, [but] do actually venture it. And so those that feel full confidence in God, are not afraid to lend to the Lord. And so, if we trust in God, we shall not be afraid to venture labour, and fighting, and watching, and suffering, and all things for him, since he has so abundantly promised to reward these things with that which will infinitely more than make up for all the losses or difficulties or sorrows we may experience in the way of duty.[37]

Laying up treasures in heaven through earthly sacrifice is simultaneously getting your heart into heaven and thus experiencing heaven on earth. Jim Eliot's famous quote was actually in this

---

[36] Ibid, 183.
[37] Ibid, 234.

context.[38] He said, "One of the great blessings of heaven is the appreciation of heaven on earth. He is no fool who gives what he cannot keep to gain what he cannot lose."[39] Eliot recognized heaven growing within his chest even as he chose a path of physical hardship for his life. As he poured himself out to others, he found that God filled him with satisfaction at an even greater rate. He discovered there's a terrific amount of earthly pleasure to be found in giving up what you're going to lose anyway. He discovered "heaven on earth" as he gave his life over to the kingdom of heaven. He saw his blessed work for what it truly was: a redeemed self-interest and a sacrificial self-service.

Christians know that "the only things we can keep are the things we freely give to God. What we try to keep for ourselves is just what we are sure to lose."[40] It must also be added that we discover a life of pleasure in giving our lives over to God. Consider, if you will, the fruit of the Spirit:

> But the fruit of the Spirit is love, joy, peace, patience, kindness, goodness, faithfulness, gentleness, self-control; against such things there is no law. Now those who belong to Christ Jesus have crucified the flesh with its passions and desires. If we live by the Spirit, let us also walk by the Spirit.
>
> *(Galatians 5:22-25)*

We acquire the fruit of the Spirit in close conjunction with the killing and crucifying of the old man and his short-sighted patterns

---

[38] Interestingly, the day before writing this, Eliot reported that he was reading of the final days of the life of David Brainerd and some of the "notations" thereof. The work in question was almost certainly *The Life and Diary of David Brainerd,* organized, annotated, and narrated by Jonathan Edwards, who anticipated the development of Christian Hedonism at every turn. Brainerd had died of tuberculosis in Edwards' home, and Edwards had collected and transcribed his journals. Edward's daughter, Jerusha, would die a few months later, having contracted tuberculosis from Brainerd.

[39] Eliot, Shadow, 108.

[40] Lewis, Mere, 168.

of thinking (cf. Romans 8:13). As the old man wanes in us, the new man has room to grow and abound. While the deeds of the flesh bring suffering to our doorstep, the fruit of the Spirit brings pleasure and satisfaction and happiness. Look over the list carefully; each and every fruit tends toward our personal satisfaction. Paul reminds us "there is no law" against seeking these sorts of personal blessings for ourselves. You should want a life of love, joy, and peace. Indeed, you're commanded to pursue such a life with all your might, hedonistically. Invest all you can in wisdom and truth, and never sell any of it (Proverbs 23:23). The fruit of the Spirit of God comes from God as a gracious gift, is a blessing to self and others and returns to God in the form of our adoration and praise. Everyone wins, and no one loses.

Ironically, it's only when we give our earthly lives over to the service of God that we actually discover the greatest pleasure in earthly things. Jeremiah Burroughs (1600-1646), the Puritan preacher, said, "Oh how sweet are all outward blessings, when we have laid them down at God's feet, and he gives us them again to enjoy."[41] When we take the time to recognize God's good favor to us in all the blessings he pours out on us, then we really begin to enjoy his blessings and to recognize them *as blessings*.

When we learn to praise him for his relentless grace unto us in the countless comforts we experience each day, the delight we take in those comforts is thereby increased a hundredfold. For example, you never really enjoy a meal to the fullest extent until you take the physical good and add to it the spiritual good of praising God for it. I have often found that while it's relatively easy to scarf down a meal with a distracted mind, without really stopping to enjoy it, a few quiet moments of sincere prayer and thanksgiving before a meal has a natural tendency to focus attention on the delight of the meal. The meal becomes an act of worship whereby I enjoy God and also enjoy the food in front of me more than I otherwise would have. To the physical pleasure I add the spiritual

---

[41] Burroughs, Self-Denial, 56%.

pleasure of praising God for the pleasure he has given me. I gain both heaven *and* earth and thus discover heaven *on* earth.

When I acknowledge earthly blessings as gifts from God, then it always feels much more like something to pause over and to savor and contemplate, as a gift from God. When all of life becomes a matter of praise and thanksgiving to God, then earth will become a heaven to you. Every Christian has an innate sense that it would be better for them to be more spiritual and more godly. That instinct is a wonderful fruit of the Holy Spirit, a pure gift from God. Follow that instinct; it is good and trustworthy and altogether satisfying.

The sacrifice God wants most from you is the "sacrifice of thanksgiving" (Psalm 50:14, 23). Thanksgiving is glorifying to God because it is an acknowledgement that God is powerful as well as gracious and good. Far from being a loss to us, however, this sort of sacrifice is a rewarding sacrifice, an endless well of personal satisfaction. Thanksgiving is pausing to recognize that a good God lies behind each of life's simple pleasures. Thanksgiving is savoring every earthly delight as an undeserved and unmerited gift from God. There is no better life on earth than a life full of thanksgiving, yet neither is there a greater sacrifice to God than thanksgiving. Thanksgiving is the purest form of worship. So blessed are those who gain heaven on earth by praising God for every earthly pleasure! So foolish are those who deny God the thanks due him, and simultaneously deny themselves the fullest enjoyment of *absolutely everything* on earth.

The Bible does not say you're supposed to give up the life of pleasure to get to heaven, but rather you're supposed to give up the life of *sinful* pleasure in order to attain the life of *true* pleasure, which is, in accordance with God's perfect design, also the path to heaven. You have to give up your worldly self-interest in favor of a redeemed self-interest. To be truly satisfied, you have to learn to hunger and thirst for righteousness rather than sin.

The question to ask yourself is not, *do I live for this life or do I live for the next?* That's entirely the wrong question (and asking the right question is always 99% of the battle). A better question would be, *should I pursue pleasure in this life through sin or through godliness today?* The answer is quite clear. The Bible promises that the life of godliness is a hundred times better life on earth. It's not living for this life *or* for the next, but rather living this life to the fullest by doing things God's way, and then discovering that the reward of a happy life is a happy eternity. You'll never discover "the good life" until you let God define it for you.

SEVERAL OBJECTIONS

Several objections must here be addressed head-on. When the Bible talks about *denying yourself* (e.g. Matthew 16:24), it doesn't mean denying yourself *pleasure*, but rather denying yourself pleasure-seeking *through sin*. "In what sense must a Christian deny himself?" asked Thomas Watson (1620-1686), the English Puritan; "I answer in general that he must deny that carnal part which is near to him as himself."[42] The Bible's self-denial is a denial of your first, sinful inclination to take the shortcut approach. It's a denial of the old man, in other words—a refusal to take moral shortcuts. Upon the same question, Thomas Manton concluded, "In short, whatsoever is of himself, in himself, belonging to himself, as a corrupt or carnal man—all that is to be denied."[43] And again, "the self which we must hate or deny is that self which stands in opposition to God, or in competition with Him, and so jostles with Him for the throne."[44]

John Piper, the American author and pastor (who coined the term "Christian Hedonism"), very insightfully noted, "Self-denial is never a virtue in itself. It has value precisely in proportion to the superiority of the reality embraced above the one denied. Self-denial that is not based on a desire for some superior goal will become the ground of boasting."[45] In commanding us to deny ourselves, God is

---

[42] Watson, Self-Denial, 9%.
[43] Manton, Self-Denial, 3%.
[44] Ibid, 4%.
[45] Piper, Desiring, 296.

not asking that we cease being *selves*, for God has made it very clear that, for better or worse, we will always be stuck with ourselves. The self we are to deny is not the self, considered absolutely, but rather the old self, the sinful self. The self we must rid ourselves of is the self that is willing to sacrifice heaven for earth (cf. Matthew 16:26). A Christian must be rigorously self-denying when it comes to sin, and yet relentlessly self-affirming in his own spiritual well-being in pursuit of the things of God.

Likewise, when the Apostle Paul said that wicked men, in the last days, will be "lovers of themselves" (2 Timothy 3:2), the context clearly indicates he is not condemning self-love, as such, but rather a worldly self-love which disregards God and seeks the destruction of others. The men in question are "lovers of self, lovers of money, boastful, arrogant, revilers, disobedient to parents, ungrateful, unholy, unloving, irreconcilable, malicious gossips, without self-control, brutal, haters of good, treacherous, reckless, conceited, lovers of pleasure rather than lovers of God" (3:2-4). Clearly, it is the *sinful* variety of self-interest and pleasure-seeking Paul has in view. Likewise, when he said love "does not seek its own" or "is not self-seeking" (1 Corinthians 13:5 NASB, NIV), he certainly wasn't saying it's wrong to pursue your own spiritual good! Again, the object in view is a sinful type of self-seeking. Love doesn't seek a sinful agenda at others' expense.[46]

Along the same lines, when Jesus talks about hating our "own life" (Luke 14:26) and our "life in this world" (John 12:25), he doesn't mean you have to automatically hate your own guts when you become a Christian. It's not your life in general you must hate, but rather your *old* life, your worldly life, your *life in this world* that

---

[46] As Edwards noted, "when it is said that charity seeketh not her own, we are to understand it of her own private good - good limited to herself. The expression, 'her own,' is a phrase of appropriation, and properly carries in its signification the idea of limitation to self. And so the like phrase in Phil. ii.21, that 'all seek their own,' carries the idea of confined and self-appropriated good, or the good that a man has singly and to himself, and in which he has no communion or partnership with another, but which he has so circumscribed and limited to himself as to exclude others" (Charity, 165).

doesn't fix its eyes on the eternal prize. You need to hate the selfish and sinful part of yourself, which inclines you to disregard God and others, because that's precisely the part of you that gets in the way of your own real, persistent, enduring pleasure.

The wicked think they are winning, but, in truth, the life of the wicked is not a life of pleasure, but rather an endlessly frustrating life of punishment (cf. 2 Peter 2:9). "The curse of the Lord is on the house of the wicked, but He blesses the dwelling of the righteous" (Proverbs 3:33). The Bible doesn't ask us to hate our own flesh, only to remove the cancer from it. The old man in you is a fool, always trading away valuable goods for mere pictures of valuable goods. "When God requires the resignation of our will [in self-denial], it is but the taking of a sword out of a madman's hands."[47] The old man in you is a bitter and unhappy man. He has unwittingly established unhappiness as his god and goal in life, and so you need to hate him and starve him and do everything you can to kill him (cf. Romans 8:13, Matthew 5:29-30). You must hate and deny yourself to the same extent you are still carrying *him* around with you; not a bit more, and not a bit less.

It may further be objected that Paul said the Apostles should be pitied more than all men if there is no resurrection from the dead (1 Corinthians 15:19). This may seem to imply that the Christian life is a pitiable sort of life if not for the fact that there is an afterlife. As noted previously, however, Paul is here responding to the belief that there is no afterlife. If there is no afterlife, Paul was travelling the world telling all sorts of lies (15:15). If there is no afterlife, every Christian has died in vain (15:18). If there is no afterlife, we might as well eat and drink and live for today (15:32). The point of view temporarily adopted by Paul here was clearly a hypothetical, pagan point of view. The perspective adopted was, as one theologian put it, "wholly imaginary."[48] If there is no afterlife,

---

[47] Manton, Self-Denial, 49%.
[48] Berkouwer, Return, 183.

then presumably there is no God and no divine promises. If there is no heaven, then certainly there are no earthly hearts in heaven.

Beyond any doubt, Paul's life was an abysmal, wasted, pitiable life from a worldly point of view. Yet no one would argue that Paul actually agreed with that perspective. He merely adopted that viewpoint temporarily to point out the hopelessness and futility of its own conclusions.[49] By his own testimony, Paul was content all of the time, in every situation (Philippians 4:12). Shall we imagine that Paul believed the wicked were more content in life than he was, when he was content *all* of the time? The life of perfect contentment in pursuit of the eternal prize may be "pitiable" from a worldly perspective, but certainly not from a Christian perspective.

The Christian life is the best possible life in a fallen world, a life of peace, joy, love, and hope. It's not a perfect life, of course. It's still life in a fallen world. Even so, it's better to have your affections set upon heaven in a fallen world than to have your heart set upon the fallen world itself. What is the Christian life but the life of Christ? And what is the life of Christ but the life God chose for himself when he dwelt among men?

Another likely objection at this point is that since I am arguing Christianity is not only a means unto eternal success, but also a means unto earthly happiness and success, my argument is a worldly-minded argument. This objection comes largely on the heels of a movement or mentality sometimes called the "Health and Wealth Gospel" (also sometimes called the "Peace and Prosperity Gospel" for those who prefer alliteration to rhyme). Basically, there have, in recent times, been scoundrels on TV who promise that if you mail them a thousand dollars, you'll miraculously get $2,000 for yourself the following week. They might even go so far as to point out that the Bible promises a hundred fold rate of return. We could easily imagine some crooked televangelist saying, "Send me a dollar,

---

[49] Paul's apologetic here seems to be a presuppositional apologetic. I explored this method of defending the faith in my short book *Evolution Evolves: A Presuppositional Apologetic Against Naturalism*. www.evolutionevolves.com

get a hundred back from God. Send me a hundred dollars, get $10,000 back from God." Christianity is here envisioned (by both parties) as a worldly get-rich-quick scheme, a sort of divine powerball lottery.

There are countless problems here. The whole spirit of such a suggestion is worldly inasmuch as the ultimate object in view—the only object in view—is earthly treasure. Worldly wealth (for its own sake) is the ultimate goal, and God simply a means to this end. We've seen this before. This is pure hypocrisy—not Christian, but anti-Christian. Such men have had their reward in full. I renounce that sort of nonsense a thousand times over. The only promise the Bible makes to the worldly is the promise of adversity.

At the same time, it must be said that there has been a tremendous overreaction on the part of many Christians to the so-called Health and Wealth Gospel. In an effort to distance themselves from its falsehoods, many have jumped from one extreme to the other and denied that Christianity offers any benefits *at all* in this life. Sometimes they even go so far as to suggest that it's sinful to be concerned about things like health and wealth. The Bible's subtle, spiritual, discerning view of health and wealth is plowed over with the bulldozer of oversimplification. Ten thousand biblical passages affirming the inherent value of health and wealth end up buried beneath the rubble.

Just as we must distinguish between a new man and an old man, a true and false desire for glory, a true and false pride, a true and false self-love, a true and false self-interest and so on, so too must we distinguish between a true and false desire for health and wealth. There is an appropriate desire for health and wealth, but also an inappropriate, inordinate desire. The old man has his reasons for desiring health and wealth, while the new man has different reasons.

The man who desires wealth should ask himself the all-important question, *why do I desire wealth?* It's a good thing to desire wealth in order to expand your program of generosity. I know one or two Christian businessmen like that, who desire more wealth in order to be a blessing to more people. That sort of wealth is good to have and good to desire (cf. Ruth 4:11). That sort of wealth is wealth without sorrow (cf. Proverbs 10:22). Such men will be greatly rewarded on account of their wealth.

Wealth is a gift directly from the hand of God, and the wisest investment we can make with it—the only investment that will last forever—is to give it right back to God by pursuing the work of Christ's kingdom. There are countless biblical affirmations that God gives generously to those who are generous to others. There's simply no way around it:

> Honor the Lord from your wealth
> And from the first of all your produce;
> So your barns will be filled with plenty
> And your vats will overflow with new wine.
>
> *(Proverbs 3:9-10)*

The reference here is to the tithes and offerings given by the tribes in Israel to the tribe of priests. The priestly tribe would go hungry if the other tribes didn't give generously, and if the priesthood went hungry, the people would no longer hear the Word preached (or see the Word preached through the daily sacrifice). God built an inherent need into the situation in Israel so that his people could lay up treasures in heaven by giving faithfully. Time and time again, God promised he would be financially faithful to those who gave faithfully to the priesthood:

> "Bring the whole tithe into the storehouse, so that there may be food in My house, and test Me now in this," says the Lord of hosts, "if I will not open for you the windows of heaven and pour out for you a blessing until it overflows. Then I will rebuke the devourer for you, so that it will not destroy the

fruits of the ground; nor will your vine in the field cast its grapes," says the Lord of hosts.

(Malachi 3:10-11)

God provides for those who provide for others, but this is, of course, a far cry from the Health and Wealth gospel. Wealth should never be an end in itself, as if the purpose of wealth was simply to store it up and hide it away. The point of wealth is not to make your fast car faster or your big house bigger; that sort of wealth is spiritual poverty. If you want to be truly rich, give it all away, and you'll have a truer, more lasting treasure in heaven. What you'll discover is that God gives generously to those who give it all away, so that they can repeat the cycle of giving (and of eternal rewards) yet again. "One who is gracious to a poor man lends to the Lord, and He will repay him for his good deed" (Proverbs 19:17).

Things are no different with health. In the Ten Commandments, God promised to bestow long life on those who honor their parents, a point reiterated in the New Testament (cf. Exodus 20:12, Ephesians 6:1-3). In fact, all of the commandments tend toward long life (cf. Deuteronomy 32:47). Clearly then, it's good to desire a long, healthy life; that's why God offers it as an incentive to us. "The fear of the Lord prolongs life, but the years of the wicked will be shortened" (Proverbs 10:27). Yet with health, as with wealth, most people's motivation for living a long life is not to honor God for as long as possible by laying up treasures in heaven for as long as possible. Rather, they turn the blessing of life into a curse for themselves by wanting to satisfy their own sinful desires for as long as possible.

Our time on earth is where we make all our important investment decisions, and it's good to want more time to invest in Christ's promised rewards. Christ died to take away all of the sins of all who hope exclusively in him. If you hope in him, there's no more punishment to be had for sin, for he paid for all of that already. All that remains for you is peace with God and endless opportunity. There's a ripe harvest as far as the eye can see (cf. Matthew 9:37). There's so much harvest, there's not enough workers to gather it all (cf. Luke 10:2). It's good to want more time to reap. Surprisingly enough, there is no better reason to eat right, exercise, and live life to the fullest than the prospect of heavenly rewards from the hand of God.

God promises us that forsaking our sin leads to a hundred-fold personal gain, both in this life and the next, but that gain can only be properly evaluated through the discerning eyes of faith. You may gain a hundred million dollars' worth of peace and joy and contentment while you give away a million dollars. The world will scoff at you and say you're a dolt and a dimwit for giving all that money away, but that's because they're not accounting for the heaven in your heart. Nor do they understand the power of God who has promised to supply all your future needs (Philippians 4:19).

We would search the Bible's pages in vain for worldly success formulas. At the same time, we don't want to jump to the opposite extreme of suggesting that a life full of sin will give us our best shot at personal fulfilment on planet earth. That is no less a falsehood. My argument is that the Christian life is a better, more blessed life on earth than the life of sin, provided we look at the whole picture, and also take into account the inward, invisible, spiritual life of man.

To be sure, Christians struggle with physical hardships and financial setbacks like everyone else, but when our hearts are in heaven, our earthly troubles certainly seem much less significant. Even Job, at the peak of indescribable suffering, could still see heavenly treasures off in the distance and could still find heaven in his heart. He smiled and whispered, "It is still my consolation and I rejoice in unsparing pain, that I have not denied the words of the Holy One" (6:10). Regardless of their physical well-being at any particular moment, "great wealth is in the house of the righteous, but trouble is in the income of the wicked" (Proverbs 15:6). There is no better life on earth than the life of a Christian. The life of faith is true life. "The reward of humility and the fear of the Lord are riches, honor and life" (Proverbs 22:4).

The old man judges by a shallow, visible standard, but he is no fool who gives what he cannot keep in order to gain what he cannot lose. According to both Jesus and Paul, the gain pertains not just to the next life but to this one as well. Those who put their treasure in heaven and set their affection upon the God of Heaven have a heart full of heaven even in this life, and that is objectively worth more than all the world's wealth. God will always fill the cup faster than you can pour it out, though oftentimes God's blessings come in subtle, spiritual forms, so as to frustrate sinful, worldly desires. God never kneels to sinful demands for worldly success formulas. We must conform to him, for it would be foolish of him to conform to us.

The person who sacrifices the life of sin to follow Christ gains the life of true pleasure in this world, and in gaining the life of true pleasure in this world, they also gain the eternal reward. A Christian clings to the immovable promises of the immovable God, and has his heart immovably in heaven, even in the midst of the ever-changing current of this life. He knows that God seeks his good in all things and all situations, and he makes the most of every situation, unto his own spiritual good. In whatever he does, he prospers (Psalm 1:3), because the game is totally rigged in his favor, as it was his heavenly Father who created the whole world for their mutual success.

In the three chapters to follow, I will argue that God's commandments to love your neighbor as yourself (cf. Mark 12:31), your spouse as yourself (cf. Ephesians 5:33), and other Christians as yourself (cf. Galatians 6:10) all encourage a redeemed sense of self-interest. I will also argue that obeying those commandments works to your own advantage, on both a short-term, earthly basis and on a long-term, heavenly basis.

LOVING YOUR NEIGHBOR
AS YOURSELF

We're presented with false dilemmas all the time in everyday life. One of my kids might say, "Hey, we could either go to McDonalds or Pizza Hut tonight," while conveniently overlooking the option of the healthy grilled salmon in the refrigerator. Or my wife might say, "Hey, you could either take me on a tropical vacation or a romantic mountain vacation," while conveniently overlooking the option of saving money by just staying home. Presenting someone with two options *as if* those were the only options available, when, in fact, there are other viable alternatives is a strategy we sometimes use to try to back someone into a corner and get what we want out of them. Students of formal logic call it the "fallacy of faulty alternatives." Fortunately, it's fairly easy to spot most of the time, especially when you learn its name and start to watch out for it.

Things get a little more complicated when the one trying to corner you with a false dilemma is yourself, because you haven't properly evaluated all of your options. For example, while we commonly feel we must decide between loving ourselves *or* loving others, I want to suggest that the Bible presents another, better option.

When the Bible says you should "love your neighbor as yourself" (Leviticus 19:18,34, Mark 12:31), the most basic meaning is that you should love everyone all the time, without making exceptions. That much seems fairly obvious. What might be less obvious is that, in commanding you to love your neighbor *as yourself,* the Bible is also commanding you to love yourself. For if it were true that you need not necessarily love yourself, and you must love your neighbor as yourself, then it would follow, of course, that you need not necessarily love your neighbor. In other words, if it were permissible to feel indifferent or apathetic about yourself, then loving your neighbor as you love yourself would imply no more than feeling indifferent and apathetic about your neighbor. This hardly seems in line with the assumptions and intentions of the commandment.

Here again, the Bible assumes it's normal to seek your own welfare and prosperity. In fact, the passage teaches that the model upon which you should base your love for your neighbor is the natural love you feel for yourself.[50] Edwards noted that the commandment "makes self-love a rule and measure by which our love to others should be regulated."[51]

Furthermore, if you are to love your neighbor as you love yourself, then certainly it also follows that you must love yourself correctly, for how can you love your neighbor as yourself correctly if you do not love yourself correctly? Augustine observed, "If you have not learned how to love yourself, I am afraid you will cheat your neighbor as yourself!"[52] To love yourself correctly is to be a Christian walking in obedience to God and doing everything you can to think God's thoughts after him. Likewise, the correct way to

---

[50] A few biblical commentators (most notably, Martin Luther) have argued that there is an implied rebuke of our self-love in the passage, as if the verse were to be read "love your neighbor as you sinfully love yourself," but this view can be seen as incorrect, in that if it were correct, we would then have to imagine that our love for our neighbors is to be *modeled upon* a sinful and faulty self-love. The passage would seemingly have to be read, "sinfully love your neighbor as you sinfully love yourself," but this is absurd. Seeing this fact, the majority of commentators have rejected this interpretation, as Jonathan Edwards does in the quote to follow.

[51] Edwards, Charity, 160.

[52] Augustine, City of God, quoted in O'Donovan, Problem, 40.

love your neighbor as yourself is to be desirous that your neighbor be of like mind with you, so as to think the same thoughts and to partake in the same spiritual blessings. "He truly loves his friend who loves God in his friend, either because God is in his friend, or that he may be so."[53]

In commanding us to love our neighbors as ourselves, we see that, far from condemning self-love, the Bible actually forbids us to choose between loving one's self or loving others, for we must love our neighbor in the same manner and to the same extent we love ourselves. The basic meaning is, "the good one wishes to happen to oneself, one must wish for the other man as well; the evil one does not wish to happen to oneself one should not wish to happen to him; this is the attitude one should adopt towards all men."[54]

Loving your neighbor as yourself implies a willingness to serve your neighbor. Even as you naturally serve yourself, because you naturally love yourself, so too you should love and serve your neighbor. Jesus said, "In everything, therefore, treat people the same way you want them to treat you" (Matthew 7:12). If you could somehow turn off your sense of self-interest, such that you no longer cared about how others treated you, Jesus' "golden rule" would no longer have any force or meaning. If you could genuinely be indifferent as to whether others treated you well or badly, then you could seemingly treat others either well or badly and still be following Jesus' commandment to treat others as you want to be treated. Clearly, this is not possible in practice. Jesus obviously assumed that all people are self-interested and cannot be otherwise, and that his golden rule was, therefore, universally applicable. It applies to all people at all times, because all people desire their own good. Once again, far from discouraging self-interest, Jesus saw self-interest as a basic, fixed fact of humanity. Self-interest wasn't

---

[53] Augustine, Sermon 336, quoted in O'Donovan, Problem, 36.
[54] Augustine, Quoted in O'Donovan, Problem, 114.

caused by sin, but merely *corrupted* by sin. The fix, therefore, isn't to destroy self-interest, but rather to redeem self-interest.

One thing that should be very obvious from Jesus' golden rule, but is often overlooked, is that you're clearly more likely to be treated well by others if you treat them well, so treating them well makes good, rational sense from a hedonistic perspective. Granted, people may abuse you whether you're nice to them or not. And granted, you have to treat them well either way, because you're ultimately looking for God's approval rather than the approval of men. Nevertheless, righteousness is never without its earthly rewards. God wants what's best for you, now and forever, and his commandments always tend toward your good. Treating others as you want to be treated gives you the very best shot of having them treat you as *you* would treat you.

Naturally, you want people to treat you well, because you're in the business of you, and that's ok; so am I. I don't know about you, but I only get to be me, and only get to walk around as myself, and only get to see the sunset through my own eyes. As far as I can tell, God made me to be me and not to be you or God or anyone else, and I don't really think it's anything to be ashamed of. In one sense at least, my life *is* about me. For better, for worse, for richer, for poorer, in sickness and in health, I'm always going to be stuck with myself.

While Jesus taught that there is an appropriate place for a redeemed self-interest and a righteous ambition, he was quick to point out that our self-interest must not be to the exclusion of others or at others' expense, because things won't work out right that way. As far as social interaction is concerned, for the most part you get what you give. When you go to war with your neighbor, obviously *you yourself* are also at war. Those who live by the sword also die by the sword (Matthew 26:52). People tend to be good to those who are good to them and bad to those who are bad to them. Your own behavior toward others will generally be echoed or reflected right back to you. Being stingy toward another man is being stingy toward yourself from a big picture perspective:

> And [Jesus] told them a parable, saying, "The land of a rich man was very productive. And he began reasoning to himself, saying, 'What shall I do, since I have no place to store my crops?' Then he said, 'This is what I will do: I will tear down my barns and build larger ones, and there I will store all my grain and my goods. And I will say to my soul, "Soul, you have many goods laid up for many years to come; take your ease, eat, drink and be merry."' But God said to him, 'You fool! This very night your soul is required of you; and now who will own what you have prepared?' So is the man who stores up treasure for himself, and is not rich toward God." ... "[Instead,] sell your possessions and give to charity; make yourselves money belts which do not wear out, an unfailing treasure in heaven, where no thief comes near nor moth destroys. For where your treasure is, there your heart will be also."
>
> *(Luke 12:16-21, 33-34)*

The rich man had a barn packed to the brim with grain, more than enough to sustain himself for the foreseeable future. He had a wonderful opportunity to be "rich toward God" by giving to those less fortunate, to let his wealth literally overflow unto his neighbors as his barn could hold no more, and to thereby lay up a lasting treasure and an eternal money belt. Oh, what joy, to have more than enough for yourself and more than enough to give to others! How many of the poor he could have blessed, and how they would have loved him and thanked God for him! Surely if he had been generous with his neighbors, and his fortunes had temporarily changed for the worse in the future, his neighbors would have remembered his generosity and taken care of him in his time of need, unto their mutual thanksgiving and praise of God.

Yet the rich man planned otherwise. He did not trust God to supply his future needs, and so he took matters into his own hands. Even while his neighbors suffered from hunger, he tore down his perfectly good barns and spent all his energy on bigger and better barns to store even more grain for himself, to ensure his perpetual leisure and wealth for years to come. He made worldly wealth his goal as though his life would last forever, as though no one else mattered at all, and as though there was no God to whom he would have to give account. He did not invest wisely, but rather invested entirely in perishable goods. And at the very moment all the sweating and toiling seemed to be finished, and it was finally time to kick back and relax—"to eat, drink and be merry"—his life was required of him. Though he tried to establish peace for himself, he never found it, for his hope and his heart was stuck in this transient world.

Notice from the parable, it's not serving self *or* serving others, but serving self *by* serving others. You get the lasting money belt by opening up the temporary money belt unto others. It's not you or your neighbor you have to choose between, but rather, you serve yourself precisely by serving your neighbor. It's what game theorists call a *non zero sum* game, a game no one has to lose, and where everyone can walk away a winner. You get a treasure in heaven by giving of your perishable, earthly treasure, and this tends also unto your own present satisfaction.

Giving your money away is obviously a sacrifice, but it's not so much a selfless sacrifice as it is a self-interested sacrifice, because you're merely trading that treasure you can't possibly keep for a treasure you'll certainly keep forever. That's just smart investing. Giving to others is setting aside some "profit" for yourself for later (Philippians 4:17).

God promised that "he who gives to the poor will never want, but he who shuts his eyes will have many curses" (Proverbs 28:27).

Jesus likewise promised "Give, and it will be given to you. They will pour into your lap a good measure—pressed down, shaken together, and running over. For by your standard of measure it will be measured to you in return" (Luke 6:38). Generosity to others honors God by demonstrating our faith and reliance upon God to provide for us in the future, and also tends to promote the immediate spiritual blessings of thanksgiving, contentment, and joy.

The question to ask yourself is not, *should I serve others today or should I serve myself,* for that sets up a faulty dilemma. The biblical paradigm is serving self through the service of others. With regard to the wealthy, Paul told the young pastor Timothy to "instruct them to do good, to be rich in good works, to be generous and ready to share, storing up *for themselves* the treasure of a good foundation for the future, so that they may take hold of that which is life indeed" (1 Timothy 6:18-19). Sacrificing your earthly treasure in the service of others is a personal sacrifice that secures your own advantage. Generosity with money is one good way to get your heart into heaven through the practical exercise of your faith. It's also a wonderful way of storing up the sort of treasure that has a good foundation for the future. Don't invest too heavily in the shifting stream of this life, but rather seek to grab hold of that life which is life indeed.

Likewise, the question is not, *should I love my neighbor or should I love myself?* It's a good thing to love yourself, but you can only love yourself correctly by including your neighbor in your self-love. By treating your neighbor as you would ideally like to be treated by him, peace between you and your neighbor has room to flourish and grow unto the betterment of the whole neighborhood. You should love your neighbor as yourself, because that's what's best *for yourself,* because you too are his neighbor, and you too have to live with the overall condition of the neighborhood. Do unto others as you would have them do unto you, because that's your best chance of having them do unto you as *you* would do unto you.

When Jesus said it's more blessed to give than to receive (Acts 20:35), he wasn't just trying to sound pious. What he had in view was the idea that you gain an eternal treasure for yourself through your earthly sacrifice. He wasn't being ironic or ascetic. It *really is* more of a blessing for you to give than to receive, since giving is more profitable to you, since the Lord himself will repay you a hundredfold for your service to him, both in this life and the next.

When we come to see earthly service and sacrifice unto others as a personal gain for ourselves, we'll be much less reluctant to help, and much more likely to jump right into action without complaining or second-guessing ourselves. When we see someone in need, we'll be the first in line to help as if it were Jesus himself who needed our aid: "Truly I say to you," said our Lord, "to the extent that you did it to one of these brothers of Mine, even the least of them, you did it to Me" (Matthew 25:45). As Thomas Manton noted, loving our neighbors is the clearest expression of loving God:

> God needs nothing from us; He is elevated far above our bounty and kindness. Therefore, it would have been easy [for us] to pretend love to God, if God had not delegated His own right upon our neighbors, and made them His agents to receive those respects, that we cannot so well bestow upon God Himself. God needs not our love, but His servants do! Therefore it is made the test of our love to God that we love our brother. "If a man say I love God, and hateth his brother, he is a liar" (1 John 4:20); if a man loves not his brother, "how dwelleth the love of God in him?" (1 John 3:17). We cannot love God aright without loving our brother, and we cannot love our brother aright if we love not God. We must love our brother for God's sake. Therefore, our pretensions are mere lies when we

pretend to be open to God, and yet our hearts are shut against our brethren.[55]

To love your neighbor is to love God (cf. Psalm 16:2-3). Giving your neighbor something as trivial as a cup of cold water out of reverence and honor for Jesus earns a heavenly reward (Matthew 10:42). Wasting a whole afternoon helping someone move or visiting someone sick must surely be worth a heavenly fortune. It may be a "waste" of an afternoon when viewed from the old man's perspective, but it's important time well-spent from the perspective of the new man and his renewed sense of self-interest. Whoever wastes his life in the right way discovers true life (cf. Matthew 16:25).

Loving your neighbor as yourself implies accounting your neighbor's successes to be your own successes:

> By love, a man's self is so extended and enlarged, that others, so far as they are beloved, do, as it were, become parts of himself, so that, wherein their interest is promoted, he believes his own is promoted, and wherein theirs is injured, his also is injured.[56]

This is the very attitude we will have toward one another in heaven, and thus adopting this heavenly attitude now is a way of getting the party started early.

Loving your neighbor as yourself implies letting go of bitterness and anger. Whoever first said "resentment is like taking poison and hoping the other person dies" was exactly right.[57] Bitterness in our own souls hinders us in our spiritual walk with God. Likewise, those who fight with others get that same

---

[55] Manton, Self-Denial, 80%.

[56] Edwards, Charity, 172.

[57] I do not know the original source of the quote. It is variously attributed to Augustine as well as several different modern authors.

aggression echoed back to them. "If you bite and devour one another," said Paul, "take care that you are not consumed by one another" (Galatians 5:15).

Sometimes we think there's some mysterious benefit in harboring bad feelings, holding grudges, and picking fights, but if you examine it closely you'll find there isn't any truth to it; it was all just sin's delusion. You should forgive others not just for their sake, but even more so for your own sake, since it hurts you just as much, if not more, than it hurts them. Some people go decades holding a grudge while the other person hasn't the faintest clue about it. Which of the two is really injured by it then? Søren Kierkegaard (1813-1855), the Danish, Christian philosopher, said, "Certainly it is terrifying and terrible when love is changed into hate, but for whom is it really terrible? I wonder if it is not most terrible for the one...within whom love has turned to hate!"[58] We should love others as we love ourselves, take a vested interest in them, and make every effort to make their journey easier.

Love your neighbor as you love yourself. The most you can love anyone is to love them as yourself (cf. 1 Samuel 18:1, 20:17). One of the great ironies of the world is that those who are greedy with their time and money and hoard it all unto themselves ultimately end up being the poorest, while those who sacrifice the most still end up with the most in the end. "Aim at heaven and you will get earth 'thrown in': aim at earth and you will get neither."[59] Most people try to shortcut the line and push others out of the way to get ahead, but really, it's those who serve others and let everyone else go first who will win the first place victory wreath. "If anyone wants to be first," said our Messiah, "he shall be last of all and servant of all" (Mark 9:35).

---

[58] Kierkegaard, Love, 49.
[59] Lewis, Mere, 112.

LOVING YOUR SPOUSE
AS YOURSELF

So husbands ought also to love their own wives as their own bodies. He who loves his own wife loves himself; *for no one ever hated his own flesh, but nourishes and cherishes it,* just as Christ also does the church, because we are members of His body.

(Ephesians 5:28-30)

Paul encouraged husbands everywhere to love their wives as they love their own bodies. Obviously, we all identify with our own bodies, so Paul's admonition is, in essence, for husbands to love their wives as they love themselves. Notice Paul's encouragement to husbands is rooted in the fact that husbands naturally love themselves. If I didn't naturally love myself, then Paul's appeal to me to love my wife as myself would simply fall on deaf ears. In this we see, once again, a very clear harmony and consistency between Paul's teaching and Jesus' teaching. Paul assumed all husbands love themselves and desire the best for themselves, because he assumed all people everywhere love themselves and desire the best for themselves. (The consummate consistency of the entire Bible on this point is a clear demonstration of its divine origin, particularly when we recall it was written by some 40 authors of diverse backgrounds over a span of nearly two millennia).

Furthermore, saying "no one ever hated his own flesh" is to say that all people everywhere desire their own good, without "ever" a single exception. God made man self-interested. It's one of the traits God hard-wired into each of us, a part of our very nature as humans.

It may be objected that some people seem to hate their own flesh, even going so far as to hurt or even kill themselves, but I think if we inspect those situations closely, we will find they were actually trying to diminish their suffering. The man who ends his life no doubt hopes to bring an end to his turmoil and pain, and, in that regard, sees suicide as the best option for himself in that moment. He gives up his life in an attempt to give up his misery. Thomas Aquinas (1225-1274), the Medieval theologian and philosopher said, "No man wills and works evil to himself, except he apprehend it under the aspect of good. For even they who kill themselves, apprehend death itself as a good, considered as putting an end to some unhappiness or pain."[60] Even suicide is an expression of self-love, however misguided it may be.

Likewise, people who purposely cut themselves generally describe it as a way to transfer a nagging emotional pain into a temporary physical pain, and thus to diminish their overall suffering. First appearances can sometimes be deceiving, but we know from the Bible that no one ever hated their own flesh, and that to be human is to be inherently self-loving. As Augustine put it, self-love is "a law of nature which has never been violated."[61]

Paul bolsters his encouragement to husbands with the interesting observation that "he who loves his own wife loves himself" (v. 28). After 14 years of marriage, I think I'm finally beginning to see Paul's point here. This seems to me to be the Apostle's positive spin on the popular truism, "If momma ain't happy, ain't nobody happy," and that other annoying expression,

---

[60] Summa Theologica, quoted in Alcorn, Happiness, 32.
[61] Augustine, On Christian Doctrine, quoted in Rogers, Anthology, 55. Augustine greatly anticipates modern science here!

"Happy wife, happy life." To put it simply, showing love to my wife has the practical effect of showing love to myself, because if I'm loving to her, she'll tend to be loving to me as well.

It's simple, practical, biblical wisdom that you reap what you sow (Galatians 6:7). Generally speaking, you get back what you put out there. If you plant corn, you get corn, whereas if you plant wheat, you get wheat. Similarly, other humans will almost always echo back what they get from you. If you plant antagonism, you'll get antagonism, whereas if you plant peace, you'll get peace. "According to what I have seen, those who plow iniquity and those who sow trouble harvest it" (Job 4:8). Nothing seems to come so naturally as calling someone an idiot when they've called you an idiot, or lazy when they've called you lazy, and the same is true of life's niceties. My momma taught me that when someone says "Have a nice day," or "It's nice to meet you," you're supposed to reflect the same right back to them.

If I get home from work and greet my wife with a random insult, her first inclination, no doubt, will be to insult me in turn, whereas if I decide instead to pay her a compliment, chances are the evening will run smoother overall. Those who bless others tend to receive a blessing in turn, and the same is true of those who throw darts at others: "[The wicked man] loved cursing, so it came to him; And he did not delight in blessing, so it was far from him" (Psalm 109:17).

In real life, it's never so simple as deciding whether or not to greet my wife with a random insult, of course. What actually happens, more realistically, is a long day at work follows a stiff neck and a restless night's sleep. The tone in my voice isn't as friendly as it could be when I get home, and I'm impatient with the kids. My greeting is curt, and I choose a few words poorly over the next hour. My wife tells me I'm grumpy at which time I draw her into a semi-scholastic debate about which of us is really the grumpy one in the relationship. (Calling attention to her logical fallacies always goes over tremendously). We begin to reflect subtle insults and darts back and forth like a game of ping pong. After a long series of ungracious interpretations of one another's often careless words, we both ultimately come to the conclusion that we each married a selfish nincompoop. I harden my heart against her, and bitterness sets in. I tell myself I'm going to make her life difficult, and I won't budge an inch from my self-righteous position in the argument until she kneels before me in tears, formal written apology in hand. It's a wonderful plan I've hatched out, except for one thing: inevitably, I have to make myself miserable to ensure my wife's misery throughout the ordeal.

Paul gives me one of the keys to escape the downward spiral: I have to see myself in my wife. I have to see my wife as an extension of myself in a certain sense, almost like part of my own body. I have to recognize that to hate her is to hate myself, and that it's better for me to love her as I love myself, because in showing love to her, I show love to myself in a very practical way. We are bound together as one in marriage—bound at the hip, as it were— and if I let bitterness take hold and start to drag her down with unloving words, for every inch I drag her down, I go right alongside for the ride. Spouse-destruction is self-destruction, and the reason I return to that well time and time again is because I'm a sinner and my sin makes me blind and stupid. Though he is losing ground, the old man and his short-sighted desires still linger within me (cf. Romans 7:14-25).

Eve was created from the rib of Adam, taken out of his own body (Genesis 2:21). In marriage, the two are brought together again as one flesh (Genesis 2:24). Husband and wife become one flesh covenantally, in legal union with one another. They become one flesh practically as they walk through life together. They become united as one flesh physically in the bedroom. They become one flesh literally when together they conceive a child, whose body is a perfectly unique combination of a perfectly unique selection of right around 50% of their individual DNA. To love your spouse is to love yourself, for you are one with your spouse in a number of both legal and practical ways.

In order to ensure my own success and happiness in marriage, I have to make a habit of loving my wife as I love myself. I have to love my wife as I love my own life or my own flesh. I have to look out for her best interest in the same manner, to the same extent that I look out for my own best interest. I have to make a habit of being gracious to her (no sense being ungracious to myself), overlooking offenses (no sense being easily offended at myself), being gentle (no sense being angry with myself), and seeking reconciliation (no sense being alienated from myself). If I can learn how to do those things, then peace has room to grow and love has room to grow exponentially, multiplying a hundredfold as the years roll on.

The trick is not to stop loving myself, and to just love my wife exclusively, as if it's really only possible for one of us to be satisfied with the relationship, but rather to let the circle of my self-love expand until it also encompasses my wife. I have committed myself exclusively to her in marriage and so I should see her as an extension of myself; her good always implies my good and her harm always implies my harm. I should think of her as my *second self* or, if you like, my *other I*. When I love her as I love myself and see her desires as my desires, I will desire her desires as my desires, and I will see her victories and defeats as my victories and defeats. I will naturally want her to win more and to lose less and I will naturally go out of my way to help her.

Early in my marriage, I turned some aspects of matrimony into a competition. For example, because of a certain worldly tendency toward laziness, I would weigh out how much work I did and how much work she did on any given day, and would want the division of labor to be split right down the middle. If I felt I had done more work than her that day, I'd want to be lazy and sit around in my undies, so as to give her an opportunity to catch up, so to speak. (I added the undie part just for effect). My calculations were always quite biased in my favor, of course. I would grade myself quite generously and be quite stingy when deciding upon her grade for the day. If I got home from the office and she asked me to help out with our young kids or to help around the house, I would commonly grumble and complain about it, since I generally reckoned myself to be ahead for the day. Without realizing it, I had established an antagonistic situation between us. I set us up as enemies in a *zero sum* game, like a football game, where only one team can win. I wouldn't help her, and would let her know—in one way or another—that I was winning for the day and so naturally, she'd echo the same sorts of sentiments back to me, each of us heading down the path of bitterness and isolation.

I remember a turning point came for me when I heard someone (though I do not remember who) on the wonderful *Focus on the Family* radio program say marriage isn't a competition, and we should serve our spouses as unto the Lord. I was deeply convicted, and I realized at that point that my worldly self-interest was self-destructive behavior. In setting her up as my enemy, I had become an enemy unto myself. Though I accounted myself the victor each day, this was in the face of constant loss and perpetual self-defeat. Upon this realization, I repented of my sin and stupidity, and the general trajectory changed from competition to cooperation, as I consciously tried to stop "keeping score." Rather than setting us up as opponents, I made it more of a point to serve her, as unto the Lord, simply by helping out more with dishes, cooking, and the like.

In a very different (though certainly related) context, the game theorist Robert Axelrod noted that, "Not being nice may look promising at first, but in the long run it can destroy the very environment it needs for its own success."[62] Seeking the destruction of another is like cutting the floor out from under yourself. If you place others outside of your affection, you almost automatically place yourself outside of theirs. To the extent I am unloving to my wife, I am also unloving to myself, since we live under the same

---

[62] Axelrod, *Evolution*, 52.

roof and endlessly parrot one another's sentiments. I have to learn to renew my mind and transform my worldly self-interest into a biblical, redeemed self-interest. I have to cry out to God, with Jim Elliot, "Reveal myself to me, that I may see what Thou dost see."[63] I have to plead, alongside Job, "That which I see not, teach thou me" (Job 34:32 KJV).

Sex is a very good analogy for everything we've been talking about, and this seems to be the place to mention it. Imagine there are two different ways to approach it. First there's the way of worldly self-interest. The old man goes into it with disregard for his wife's pleasure, because his concern for himself doesn't encompass his wife. It makes no real difference to him whether she likes it or not, because he doesn't see her as an extension of himself, and because he's really not that concerned about the future, only the present. He wants his reward sooner rather than later. For lack of a better way of putting it, he's all, "wham, bam, thank-you ma'am."

Now on a very short timeline, this may work out somewhat decently for him. But how's it going to work out in the long run? Probably not very well, because next time his wife's going to remember the whole "wham, bam" incident, and it's not very likely she's going to be interested in a repeat; probably she'd rather just try to blot the whole thing out of her memory.

I'd bet good money (in fact, I'd bet everything I own without a second thought) that there are a whole lot of men who can't figure out why their wives aren't more interested in them, when one gigantic reason is that they disregard their wives' pleasure and make her feel more like an unpaid hooker than an equal partner. More or less, their wives echo back to them the level of satisfaction they received (by opting for abstinence or something close to it), and so things tend toward stagnation.

The other way to approach it is, of course, the smarter way, the way of redeemed self-interest. The new man tries to think with a more long-term vision. He takes a much more indirect approach

---

[63] Eliot, *Shadow*, 69.

to his own satisfaction. He tries to treat her as he would want to be treated. He tries to see her desires as his own desires. He tries to figure out what she likes, and he makes her pleasure the priority. Obviously, that's going to work out best for her, and it's also going to tend to work out best for him in the long run, because she's naturally going to be much more likely to want to get together again sometime in the near future. Ideally, the marriage bed is the place where two people seek the good of the other (seek even to outdo one another in seeking the good of the other), and if it's working anything like it should, nobody will be losing out and everyone will be winning, precisely as it should be, precisely as God intended.

Now ask yourself this question: what would *selfless* sex look like? Would I do my best not to like it? Would I ask for forgiveness each time it felt a little bit good, since my life is not about me and I'm not to be selfish in such a manner? It would be nothing short of comical insanity trying to imagine a person who tried to deny their own pleasure in sex. It's obvious God designed sex to be pleasurable to us, and that the prospect of pleasure is what drives us to pursue it in the first place. It would be only a modest exaggeration to say, if not for sex, all men would be perpetual bachelors.

We need to be crystal clear that there's nothing wrong with desiring pleasure. God made pleasure, and, believe it or not, pleasure is actually designed to be pleasurable! Nor is there anything wrong with loving your spouse on account of the pleasure they bring you (sexual or otherwise); that's normal, natural, and good. A spouse is a tremendous personal blessing. "He who finds a wife finds a good thing and obtains favor from the Lord" (Proverbs 18:22). The problem is not that sex is pleasurable to self-interested people, but rather that people pursue their own pleasure to the exclusion of others and often in sinful contexts, outside of the covenant-relationship sanctioned by God (cf. 1 Corinthians 6:9-11).

We see again that while everyone seeks their own good and their own pleasure, there are two very different ways to go about it.

85

There's a worldly self-interest that takes its reward sooner rather than later and focuses only on the immediate gain. The old man takes a short-sighted, shortcut, smash-and-grab approach to personal satisfaction. The new man, on the other hand, adopts a more intelligent vision that seeks the long-term good through the short-term sacrifice. The great irony (the secret, if you will) is that the long-term vision also works out better for me in the short-term.

Getting back to the original passage, Paul doesn't describe a situation in which one party must disregard their own self-interest for the good of the other, but rather Paul describes seeking satisfaction for yourself *through* love of another. To love your wife is to love your own life. We should each see ourselves in the other and thus pursue the other's satisfaction to the fullest extent possible, and the more we do that, the more we'll each tend to reap the benefits. When I see myself in my wife, my natural inclination will be to put her first, because she is the first *me* that comes into my field of vision. I will see her desires as my desires, and I will try to fulfill them, because I always want to see my desires fulfilled. If we can each learn how to seek the other's good to the same extent we seek our own good, then it will seem as though heaven has begun on earth for both of us.

The more we sacrifice for one another, the more we'll each be inclined to sacrifice for one another, and the more the general course of our marriage will tend toward health rather than sickness. Since we will each be willing to go out of our way to help one another, we will seem to one another to be quite selfless even though, in reality, we are each just self-interested in a sensible, God-honoring way. We will have discovered the great secret of sacrificial self-service.

"Each individual among you," said Paul, "is to love his own wife even as himself" (Ephesians 5:33). Loving your spouse as yourself, on account of your trust in God and his counsel for your life, has the practical effect of increasing your satisfaction in both God and your spouse, and so everyone wins and no one loses. We honor God by seeking his blessings for ourselves, and showering us with blessings costs God nothing whatsoever, for no matter how many blessings he pours out on us, his infinite power remains always exactly the same as it was previously. No matter how forcefully God exerts himself for his glory and our good, his power remains altogether undiminished. It's not wrong to love God because God does you good; it's righteous (cf. Psalm 30:1, Psalm 116:1-2).

The Bible reminds us that spouses, just like everyone else, respond better to being treated well than they do to being treated poorly. Very simple, practical, biblical insights like this can yield a tremendous harvest of peace in your life. Seeking peace with someone else always entails seeking peace for yourself as well, and the same rule applies to love, friendship, mercy, grace, and so on. This should be obvious to us from day one, but sin has a way of making us miss the obvious. It's like the mess in your own house that a visitor notices, but you yourself cannot see because you've grown so entirely accustomed to it.[64] The Bible, however, has a way of seeing every angle and cutting straight through all the nonsense that tends to cloud our vision. It cuts right to the heart of the matter, all the way down to the bone (Hebrews 4:12). The Bible is the most sensible book on planet Earth, the only book ever written without any sin-clouded vision in it.

---

[64] I'm pretty sure I lifted the metaphor from Lewis.

LOVING OTHER CHRISTIANS AS YOURSELF

All Christians are covenantally united to Christ, in a relationship that the Bible often compares to the marriage covenant between husband and wife. Just as husband and wife are legally bound together as one in marriage, so too all Christians are legally bound together as one with Christ. We have already seen this comparison in the last chapter, as we looked at Paul's teaching to the Ephesians. We nourish and cherish our bodies "just as Christ also does the church, because we are members of His body" (5:29).

The Bible gives us plenty of clues that it's not merely a happy accident that marriage bears certain striking similarities to the legal covenant relation between Christ and his church. Rather, God designed marriage to specifically represent and reflect that relation. Though marriage existed in the Garden of Eden before the fall,[65] and before anyone actually needed to be redeemed, God nevertheless had full knowledge of the redemption that would ultimately be required and he modeled the covenant union of marriage upon our future covenant union with Christ. According to Paul, the striking parallel between husband and wife in marriage and Christ and the Christian in the church was concealed or hidden in

---

[65] Genesis 3:6 indicates that Adam was Eve's "husband" prior to the fall.

the Old Testament era, but now the hidden mystery has been revealed to us by Christ (cf. Ephesians 5:25-32).[66]

After being reborn of God spiritually, we enter into this covenant-union by faith. We place our hope and trust in Jesus for the forgiveness of sin. We covenant to be faithful to him. God justifies us, which is to say he pronounces us just and sinless in a perpetually-binding legal sense on account of Christ's sacrifice. Like the wedding ring on our finger, we receive the Holy Spirit as the formal seal or pledge of our eternal union with Christ (cf. Ephesians 1:13, 2 Corinthians 5:5). We become Jesus' bride and the Father warmly invites us into the family as his legally adopted children (cf. Romans 8:15, Galatians 4:5). All who enter into covenant with Christ exercise a faithful fidelity to him by sincerely trying to obey him (cf. John 14:15).

Unlike earthly marriages, our perfect marriage bond with Christ can never be severed. Divorce is a great evil, the result of sin (cf. Leviticus 21:7, Mark 10:11-12). "'I hate divorce,' says the Lord, the God of Israel" (Malachi 2:16). Jesus will never turn from his beloved bride. He considered his heavenly family closer to him even than his earthly family (cf. Matthew 12:46-50). Blood may be thicker than water, but *Church* is thicker even than blood.

Paul draws several important implications from this. If Christ views each Christian as one with him in an important legal sense, something like an unbreakable, eternally-binding marriage union, then every Christian should also view every other Christian as being united as one with himself. We should look at one another as extensions of ourselves in a certain sense, something like the various organs of a single body:

> For even as the body is one and yet has many
> members, and all the members of the body, though
> they are many, are one body, so also is Christ. For

---

[66] See also Ephesians 5:25-27, 2 Corinthians 11:2, Revelation 19:7-9, Revelation 21:1-2.

by one Spirit we were all baptized into one body, whether Jews or Greeks, whether slaves or free, and we were all made to drink of one Spirit.

For the body is not one member, but many. If the foot says, "Because I am not a hand, I am not a part of the body," it is not for this reason any the less a part of the body. And if the ear says, "Because I am not an eye, I am not a part of the body," it is not for this reason any the less a part of the body.... But God has so composed the body, giving more abundant honor to that member which lacked, so that there may be no division in the body, but that the members may have the same care for one another. And if one member suffers, all the members suffer with it; if one member is honored, all the members rejoice with it.

(1 Corinthians 12:12-16, 24-26)

God designed our bodies such that trillions of unintelligent, unconscious cells all work together in perfect harmony as a single self-interested person. We may naturally think less of some parts of our body than others, but if any particular part causes us pain, we will quickly tend to that part. We may go decades without thinking much about our back left top molar, but after it's been throbbing for a few hours, we will not be able to focus on much besides it. We will direct our whole body to the dentist in order to tend to the one small member. We will focus the whole of our energy on helping the molar, as if the molar were the most honorable member of all, because we understand intuitively that helping the molar is helping ourselves. I like the way one Puritan put it:

In the natural body, there is no disaster that happens to any one member but all the rest are affected also. The tongue cries out when we tread upon the toe...or if the foot be pricked with a thorn, the rest of the members will testify their compassion. The tongue complains, the eyes shed tears, the head considers how to remove the thorn, and the hands provide assistance.[67]

We should think about fellow Christians in the same manner, for, in Christ, we have all become united as a single body. To aid a fellow Christian is to show concern for one's own body, and that for a number of reasons.

In the first place, the church is a great safeguard against the outside forces of evil that try to rob us of our spiritual blessings. What Jean-Jacques Rousseau (1712-1778), the Genevan Philosopher, said of secular state government is equally true of the church. In giving himself over to the corporate body, a person "gains an equivalent for everything he loses, and an increase of force for the preservation of what he has."[68] Though perhaps not without some qualification, there may be one or two other parallels between the church, as envisioned by Paul, and the state as envisioned by Rousseau:

> As soon as this multitude is so united in one body, it is impossible to offend against one of the members without attacking the body, and still more to offend against the body without the members resenting it. Duty and interest therefore equally oblige the two contracting parties to give each other help; and the same men should seek to combine, in their double capacity [as a member of the community and defender of others], all the advantages dependent upon that capacity.[69]

---

[67] Manton, Self-Denial, 83%.
[68] Rousseau, Contract, 391.
[69] Rousseau, Contract, 392.

The church is a family that exists to glorify the Sovereign; we stand united and opposed to all forces that seek to diminish or distract or divert attention away from his fame, honor, or significance. On our own, we can't accomplish all that much, but together we are the world's most powerful force; all the cities of the world and all the gates of hell will not prevail against us (Matthew 16:18). Church is the place we go to seek accountability for ourselves and to safeguard against wandering off on our own into peril. A person who avoids the public gathering of Christ's church does not rightly understand that he is neglecting his own body, as it were, unto his own spiritual malnourishment (cf. Proverbs 18:1).

Church is also a veritable treasure trove of opportunity to lay up spiritual rewards in the service of Christ's beloved. During the course of his extensive missionary journeys, the Apostle Paul took up a collection for the benefit of the impoverished saints in Jerusalem. He noted that giving to the impoverished Christians in Jerusalem was a good way for the other churches to gain heavenly "credit" or "profit" in their own accounts (Philippians 4:17 NASB, NIV). He also noted a particularly praise-worthy, hedonistic eagerness among the Macedonian Christians:

> Now, brethren, we wish to make known to you the grace of God which has been given in the churches of Macedonia, that in a great ordeal of affliction their abundance of joy and their deep poverty overflowed in the wealth of their liberality. For I testify that according to their ability, and beyond their ability, they gave of their own accord, *begging us with much urging for the favor of participation* in the support of the saints, and this, not as we had expected, but they first gave themselves to the Lord and to us by the will of God.
>
> *(2 Corinthians 8:1-5)*

The Macedonians begged Paul for a big favor. Though facing severe persecution and poverty, they knew a good investment when they saw one, and they didn't want to miss out. It wasn't a hedge fund or a hot new start-up they had in view, but rather the spiritual investment they perceived in the charitable support of their fellow saints in Jerusalem. They wanted to invest in heaven by giving their earthly money to others. Paul seems to have resisted them on account of their own deep financial need, but they persisted in pleading with him until they wore him down. It was because of the "grace of God" they were able to see the spiritual reality of the situation and invest so eagerly.

Though it would seem to be something of a logical impossibility to invest even "beyond their ability," God, in his grace to them, no doubt continued filling up the cup of generosity that they poured out unto others. Perhaps they were repeatedly surprised by windfalls and unexpected funds, which they again promptly and joyously handed to Paul for the Jerusalem saints. They were so spiritually minded they thought Paul was doing them a big favor by taking their money. That might strike us as crazy, but, in truth, they saw things clearly, and we're the ones who are crazy. For who can even begin to imagine the wealth these Macedonians possess today? "Let's not become discouraged in doing good, for in due time we will reap, if we do not become weary. So then, while we have opportunity, let's do good to all people, and *especially* to those who are of the household of the faith" (Galatians 6:9-10). Rejoicing in the prosperity of another Christian is simultaneously magnifying the Lord (cf. Psalm 35:27).

Helping a fellow Christian is helping yourself. To modify the body analogy a bit, if I sing in the choir, it would be foolish to hope that another member of the choir choke during the performance, because if one member fails, the choir fails, and I am a member of the choir. I should hope for their success and cheer them on, just as they should hope for my success and cheer me on, since I am no less in the choir than they, and they no less than I.

When they succeed, I rejoice in their accolades, because I share, in some measure, in their glory. When one of them loses their voice, I run swiftly for the honeyed tea to ensure their quick recovery, because the choir will not be as strong without them. I win through their victories, so I want them to win without fail, to win every single time out. When everyone in the church sees everyone else's wins as their own wins, then, as one overzealous politician put it, "we're going to win so much, you're going to be so sick and tired of winning."

Paul seems to have commonly thought of younger, less mature Christians as his own children. The young preacher, Timothy, for example, was his "true child in the faith" (1 Timothy 1:2). Timothy wasn't literally Paul's child, of course, but was nevertheless his "true" child, leaving us again with the impression that the church family is a truer family than any earthly family. The bond among earthly families can be broken, but the marriage bond among the heavenly family can never be broken. The Apostle John likewise referred to his Christian readers, affectionately, as his "little children" (cf. 1 John 2:1,12).

In my experience (which is, I suspect, the common experience of parents everywhere), loving my own children seems to be one of the easiest and most natural things in the world to do because they're such a clear reflection of me. They're literally made in my image (cf. Genesis 5:3), begotten of me, from my very own genetic material. They look like me, they talk like me, and they even do a lot of the same immature things I do.

I can only assume a mother must feel this to an even greater extent, as the baby was physically united to her and concealed within her own body for a time. It's remarkably easy to want to see your own children succeed because you see yourself in them in a very literal way, and thus find it completely effortless to see life through their eyes in a certain sense, living vicariously through them.

Kids cost a lot of money, of course, and they don't add anything to your being, as such, but nevertheless, "the love of the father for his children repays him for the care he takes of them."[70] Parents delight in their children's delight because they see it as their own delight in a vicarious, substitutionary sense, for they naturally see their children as an extension of themselves. To a large extent, their children's delight is accounted their own delight and their children's struggles are accounted their own struggles. A parent will sacrifice most anything for their children because of this natural sense of identity with them. This God-given instinct is so strong in us that even very immoral people still treat their children, for the most part, as they would want to be treated. They desire to see their own children succeed because they see themselves, as in a mirror, reflected in their children.

We should think of our fellow Christians in the same way. In a trillion years, you'll know the name and life story of every single saint in heaven. You'll know some of the ways Christ worked sanctification in them during their life, and some of the ways they sacrificed for him. You'll know their all-consuming love for Christ and their endless zeal for his glory. You'll see that all of their personal failings and shortcomings are long gone and that their prior failures have somehow transformed into great personal strengths. Whatever differences you had with any of them will be a distant memory, something to laugh about over a cup of coffee (which will almost certainly be the best cup of coffee you've ever tasted, though you've had trillions of cups before). You'll rejoice in their joy, and you'll rightly praise and honor them in their love toward God, just as they rightly praise and honor you in your love toward God, even as you both praise and honor God together with all your strength. You'll see Christ in them, and they'll see Christ in you, and you'll love one another for it forever and ever.

---

[70] Rousseau, Contract, 388.

BLESSED PERSECUTION

Several times now we have seen that true glory and honor are not discovered in the places we're first inclined to look. We often judge by superficial, visible standards because we fail to discern the invisible, spiritual dimensions of the world around us. We fail to think God's thoughts and so too we fail to do his deeds. Jesus' teaching often contained a great deal of irony as a result of this inversion of worldly expectation. This is nowhere more evident than in Jesus' teaching on persecution. The message on this occasion could have been entitled "Congratulations on Persecution":

> Blessed are you when people insult you and persecute you, and falsely say all kinds of evil against you because of Me. Rejoice and be glad, for your reward in heaven is great; for in the same way they persecuted the prophets who were before you.
>
> *(Matthew 5:11-12)*

If you are persecuted for being a Christian, then congratulations are in order. In the first place, congratulations are in order because you're a Christian, and that's no small matter. In the second place, congratulations are in order for being a distinguished Christian, such that the wicked desire your harm. The deeds of a Christian are an aroma of life to other Christians, but to non-Christians, a

Christian's good works smell like death (2 Corinthians 2:16), because they remind them of the sin they refuse to fully confront.

When we become Christians, we begin to judge every situation according to an invisible, spiritual standard, and we will inevitably seem absurd and even unkind to those who judge by a strictly visible, worldly standard. Kierkegaard offered a helpful analogy:

> When a strictly brought-up child is together with naughty or less good children and does not want to join them in their mischief, which they themselves, for the most part, at least, do not regard as mischief—would the naughty children know how to explain this otherwise than that the child must be a strange and foolish child? They do not see that the situation permits a quite different explanation, that the strictly brought-up child, wherever it is, continually has with him the parents' standards for what it may and may not do. If the parents were visibly present so the naughty children could see them, they would better understand the child, especially if the child appeared sad because of having to obey the parents' orders, for then it would be obvious that the child would more than willingly do as the naughty children did, and it would be easy to perceive, in fact, to see, what is holding the child back. But when the parents are not present, the naughty children cannot understand the strictly brought-up child. They think like this: either this child must not like what we other children like but [this] is silly and strange, or [else] it has the same likes but does not dare [partake]—but why doesn't it dare? The parents are not here. See, here again it is silly and strange. Consequently one cannot promptly call it badness or spite on the part of these children

when they judge the strictly brought-up child in this way. No, according to their own lights they perhaps mean very well by it. They do not understand the strictly brought-up child; no, they themselves think well of their naughtiness, and therefore they want the child to join them and be a real boy—just like the others. The application of this picture is easy. The world just cannot get into its head...that a Christian should not have the same inclinations and passions the world has.[71]

When you demonstrate love to the world by calling attention to the folly of its ways by refusing to partake in its variety of fun and its variety of self-interest, the world will inevitably perceive your love as hatred and your humility as pride. The wicked walk a path that seems true and correct to them, and do not understand they're walking the pathway of death (cf. Proverbs 14:12). "They are surprised that you do not run with them into the same excesses of dissipation, and they malign you" (1 Peter 4:4). Your old friends will think you're being selfish for refusing to walk the wide road beside them. Even so, it's truly a blessing to be a Christian of such caliber as to be a constant reminder to others of the foolishness and futility of sin, for nothing but good things awaits such a person.

In the third place, congratulations are in order because persecution is, in truth, a wonderful opportunity to lay up some tremendous heavenly treasures. Even in trials and persecution, you can rationally "rejoice and be glad," because perseverance in doing good despite persecution yields a tremendous eternal gain. Your great consolation in persecution lies in the fact that "your reward in heaven is great" for suffering hardship on account of Christ. By taking heed of this teaching, a true hedonist can turn even the most dire of situations into a blessing for himself.

---

[71] Kierkegaard, Love, 195-196.

Imagine you've been in heaven a million years and you think back to the time you faced persecution on earth. You did the right thing in the midst of others all doing the wrong thing, and endured the trial in integrity. Though the world was cruel to you, you did not echo it back to them, but tried your best to win them over through love. When they slapped you, you did not retaliate, but offered the other cheek to be slapped as well (Luke 6:29).[72] You know that trial in your short little life on earth (a mere blip on the radar of your million-year existence) led ultimately to the everlasting recollection that you stood strong and won the race and received the crown of righteousness in the face of persecution. You understand that your lot in heaven is forever better because of that trial than if you had never gone through it. Would you resent the trial at that point? Of course not! It would seem entirely insignificant, a mere nothing. That moment of pain was almost instantly translated into an eternity of pleasure and glory. As Paul proclaimed, "the sufferings of this present time are not worthy to be compared with the glory that is to be revealed to us" (Romans 8:18). If you could have a redo of your life, you'd make sure you were that much better a Christian, so you could face that much more persecution, so you could lay up that much more glorious treasure unto eternity. You'd see persecution for what it really is: a true blessing. You'd invest in it; you'd make persecution your business. You'd be so much like Christ, they'd have to kill you too.

The Bible gives us wisdom to live our lives the first time as if it were our second time around. Jesus looked at everything from a divine perspective, and he really meant it when he said "blessed are you" when you're insulted and maligned and persecuted by the

---

[72] "Turn the other cheek" seems to have implied more than just simply passivity. It's not just turning your other cheek *away* from the offender but actually turning it toward them for another round. The first century Christian treatise known as the "Didache" reads "If any man smite thee on the right cheek, turn *to him* the other cheek also, and thou wilt be perfect" (Quoted in Nygren, Agape, 258). The biblical context also seems to suggest this, for, in the same context, Jesus said if someone steals your coat, you should go the extra mile of giving them your shirt as well. Also see Isaiah 50:6.

wicked. Everything that happens to a Christian is ultimately all for their good (Romans 8:28), and persecution is especially good because it presents a very unique opportunity to lay up a very great treasure. I'm not at all suggesting you should go out and try to be a nuisance to people. Rather, I'm suggesting a serious Christian, seriously pursuing the invisible rewards of the invisible God, will always draw serious criticism from the world, which always judges by sight.

There is an astonishing example of rejoicing in persecution in the book of Acts. Not long after Jesus' ascension into heaven, Peter led the charge in beginning to preach the good news of the forgiveness of sin through the promised Messiah. He started in the capital city of Jerusalem, and this quickly got him into trouble. Along with John, he was arrested by the Jewish authorities, and:

> After calling the apostles in, they flogged them and ordered them not to speak in the name of Jesus, and then released them. So they went on their way from the presence of the Council, rejoicing that they had been considered worthy to suffer shame for His name. And every day, in the temple and from house to house, they kept right on teaching and preaching Jesus as the Christ.
>
> *(Acts 5:40-42)*

Before I was a Christian Hedonist, I found this passage quite perplexing.[73] Why on earth would someone take joy in getting beaten up? I tended to interpret it mystically, as if God magically shot down an invisible lightning bolt of joy to them to help them through the ordeal, and they were able to rejoice because of this supernatural assistance. I see now that this was a very wrong interpretation of the passage. They didn't rejoice *despite* the ordeal

---

[73] My book *Freedom From Virtual Slavery* details my "conversion" to Christian Hedonism.

but because of the ordeal. They rejoiced that they had been considered worthy to suffer an extraordinary trial for Jesus' sake. They rejoiced because they had remained faithful through the ordeal and had won for themselves a great reward.

From a Christian Hedonist perspective, this makes good, rational sense. It was quite reasonable for them to rejoice in the extraordinary ordeal, inasmuch as they understood that by enduring an extraordinary trial in faithful integrity, they had laid up an extraordinary treasure. Through the eyes of faith, they saw their reward as an absolute certainty and, therefore, a present reality. The suffering was over, nothing but a few bruises and a memory, but the glory would endure forever. The beating was seen as an occasion for rejoicing. They were able to rejoice in the here and now of this life as they looked upon their reward off in the distance.

The Apostles had taken a three-year intensive study course in Christian Hedonism under Jesus' instruction, and they applied it logically, correctly, and appropriately. They just kept on doing what they had been persecuted for, as if to say that though their bodies were bruised, their hearts were still in heaven. They were ready to make further good investments in their own future by submitting unto further suffering for the sake of Christ and his gospel of forgiveness. They knew they were blessed because they were persecuted for their faith. Peter would later encourage others to rejoice in persecution:

> Beloved, do not be surprised at the fiery ordeal among you, which comes upon you for your testing, as though something strange were happening to you; but to the degree that you share the sufferings of Christ, keep on rejoicing, so that at the revelation of His glory you may also rejoice and be overjoyed. If you are insulted for the name of Christ, you are blessed, because the Spirit of glory, and of God, rests upon you.
>
> *(1 Peter 4:12-14)*

Every Christian is united with Christ both in their suffering on earth and in their exaltation in heaven; those who are humiliated with Christ and for Christ will also "rejoice and be overjoyed" alongside Christ when he returns, for the same Spirit that rested on him also rests on them, as a "down payment" on heaven (Ephesians 1:14 CEB). As Christians, we can and should just "keep on rejoicing" in the here and now of persecution, not wasting time feeling sorry for ourselves, but rather recognizing that our consolation prize is nothing short of an eternity of unending pleasure with Christ. "Be strong and do not lose courage, for there is reward for your work" (2 Chronicles 15:7). A Christian with this mindset has his heart in heaven, beyond the reach of would-be persecutors. God "sets the needy securely on high away from affliction" (Psalm 107:41). Their hearts are in heaven, out of reach of danger:

> He that has established such a spirit and disposition of mind that the injuries received from others do not exasperate and provoke him, or disturb the calmness of his mind, lives, as it were, above injuries, and out of their reach. He conquers them, and rides over and above them, as in triumph, exalted above their power. He that has so much of the exercise of a Christian spirit, as to be able meekly to bear all injuries done him, dwells on high, where no enemy can reach him.[74]

The author of the book of Hebrews encouraged his readers to remember the confidence they formerly showed as they faced serious, sustained persecution:

> Remember the former days, when, after being enlightened, you endured a great conflict of

---

[74] Edwards, Charity, 86.

sufferings, partly by being made a public spectacle through reproaches and tribulations, and partly by becoming sharers with those who were so treated. For you showed sympathy to the prisoners and *accepted joyfully the seizure of your property*, knowing that you have for yourselves a better possession and a lasting one. Therefore, do not throw away your confidence, which has a *great reward*.

(Hebrews 10:32-35)

Taking delight in the seizure of your property is as unthinkable to the world as taking joy in getting beat up, but here the biblical author explicitly notes the rational incentive and source of motivation. The loss of physical property due to their Christian confession was seen as an investment in heavenly real estate. A person walking by faith rests confidently upon God's strength and secure in God's promises. He knows it's not a loss, but rather a trade-in and a trade-up. He looks with spiritual eyes, from the biblical and divine perspective, and he rightly perceives that he just traded the double-wide in for a mansion. As a result of their outstanding faith, their hearts were filled with joy even while their homes were being plundered. Standing confidently in God in the face of the trial yielded a "great reward" (v. 35) both at this time (in the present peace and joy) and in the age to come (in the heavenly reward).

Earlier we said everyone in heaven will be blessed with every good thing, and be entirely satisfied, though not everyone will be blessed with every pleasure to the same degree. All of God's people go to the same heaven, and yet heaven will not be exactly the same for everyone. I find it interesting that the trade-up here seems to be envisioned as of the same kind—property for property. They joyfully accepted the seizure of their property for the sake of a "better possession" presumably in the form of heavenly real estate.

If you'll entertain a bit of speculation, perhaps those areas we are faithful in on earth are met with corresponding rewards in heaven. God says to his faithful ones, "'Well done, good and faithful slave. You were faithful with a few things, I will put you in charge of many things; enter into the joy of your master'" (Matthew 25:23). This could very well imply the rewards given in heaven bear a natural correlation to the things we were faithful with on earth. For example, perhaps a person who is very faithful to God with money, but less faithful in encouraging others is blessed greatly in heaven with wealth of some sort, but less so with intimate friendships. They will still be entirely satisfied in both areas, of course, but still it would be true to say they could have been more satisfied in both areas had they been more faithful in both areas.

It would seem both reasonable and just if God blessed us more in heaven in those areas in which we were more faithful to him on earth. It has been a helpful and productive thought to me personally to consider the possibility that, if I cling to some sin on earth, my heaven will be less good in that particular area. In this way, I've tried to leverage my love of this or that sin *against itself* and so use it as a motivation to stop that sin. I try to keep in mind that every sin has a corresponding righteous pleasure. I also try to keep in mind the goal is never to turn off the desire for pleasure, but rather to refocus it upon a proper object. By pursuing my pleasure in that particular area in a righteous way rather than a sinful way, I try to ensure that I get the best version of that particular pleasure both in heaven and on earth. I offer the idea for your consideration, at any rate, as I have found it helpful.

Getting back to the main point, times of trial and persecution are times of testing, where God helps us to see the sin that remains in us. As Thomas Manton said:

> God might have translated us to heaven presently, without trouble, but there is a method in all His works. He might have caused the earth to bring forth bread as well as an ear of corn, but instead He

would have it first to grow, then to lie threshed, then ground, then baked, and so fitted for man's use. In the same way, there are many preparative changes to fit us for heaven, as the stones were squared before they were set in the temple. He is a madman that should expect his bread to grow out of the ground before the corn were cleansed by the thresher, bruised by the mill-stone, or baked in an oven... In the same way, it is a great madness to think to go to heaven without changes and afflictions. We must expect through much tribulation to enter into the kingdom of God (Acts 14:22).[75]

Trials are a refining fire in the life of a Christian. Trials are one of the ways God weans us from our sin, unto the production of more blessed spiritual fruit. He disciplines those he loves (Proverbs 3:12, Hebrews 12:6). God uses trials as opportunities to unsettle us and to help us spot secret sins and messes that may otherwise have gone unnoticed. God uses trials to show us our own weakness and inability to overcome sins and obstacles without him, and thus to encourage us to tap into his sufficiency through prayer.

A failed trial presents us with an opportunity to repent, and to grow in spiritual discernment by exercising greater attentiveness to God's Word. A trial overcome, however, is a great reward and investment in ourselves, the laying of a firm foundation where it really counts.

Sometimes a Christian doing the right thing reeks of death even to those who were formerly closest to him in his past life of sin. Oftentimes, persecution and trials come from within the boundaries of our own families and even our own churches, and remain lifelong thorns in our side. You might find your Christian sacrifice met with a scoff or a slap or a stab in the back, and, believe

---

[75] Manton, Self-denial, 58%.

me, I know how tempting it is to want to echo it right back to them seven-fold rather than turning the other cheek. Yet this worldly mindset never worked out well for anyone, because retaliation never breeds anything except more retaliation. Retaliation just escalates the neighborhood war and causes more suffering for everyone involved. Instead, you can overcome the trial of a bad neighbor, a bad boss, a bad spouse, or even a bad pastor by recognizing it for what it really is: a golden opportunity.

Paul even went so far as to encourage slaves to work hard for their masters "as for the Lord" because "from the Lord you will receive the reward" (Colossians 3:23, 24). To be clear, the Bible nowhere condones slavery. The Bible regards slavery as an evil, and simply provides guidance to mitigate that evil. For example, a Hebrew slave was automatically released after seven years of service (Exodus 21:2). A slave who received a physical injury as the result of his master's abuse was automatically to be set free (Exodus 21:26-27). The Bible nowhere commends slavery and everywhere wards against it. (Personally, I assume that without the Bible's very forceful affirmation that all men are created equal, slavery would still be in full effect today).

Even a slave with a bad master could still find solid, rational justification for working hard, because he could do it as working unto the Lord. A slave working hard for a bad master, for God's sake, would receive a greater reward than a slave who worked hard for a good master, because the former more clearly demonstrated that he did it on account of God and God's promises, because there was little earthly good in it for himself.[76]

Buckling down and serving others even when they don't deserve it and don't reciprocate should be viewed as valuable service to God. "If when you do what is right and suffer for it you patiently endure it, this finds favor with God" (1 Peter 2:20) Over

---

[76]It should go without saying that this does not, in any way, justify the oppression of another person, as if you were creating opportunities for them by persecuting them, and somehow doing it "for their own good."

time, you'll almost always see positive results in the other person's behavior as you willfully sacrifice for them, but even if you don't, you can still rejoice in the Lord that you've been presented with a unique opportunity to lay up some special rewards for yourself. You need not despair, but rather to preach this encouraging word to yourself in your trials: "the eyes of the Lord move to and fro throughout the earth that He may strongly support those whose heart is completely His" (2 Chronicles 16:9).

A couple of Jesus' apostles asked to sit right next to him in heaven, in the highest positions of honor, but Jesus said those spots were already reserved for others (Mark 10:35-40). Probably those spots are reserved for battered spouses and beaten slaves who, despite overwhelming obstacles and externally miserable lives, stood firmly planted with their hearts in heaven, full of joy and thanksgiving, who worked with all diligence as unto the Lord despite their worldly obstacles. I think it highly unlikely that the world's prominent men will occupy any of those choice spots, "for the one who is least among all of you, this is the one who is great" (Luke 9:48).

Notice that in telling us the least (in some sense) will be the greatest (in some other sense), Jesus was clearly assuming it's natural for us to want to be great, and was actually encouraging us to be great. You should want to be called great in the kingdom of heaven (cf. Matthew 5:19). The key to becoming the greatest, however, isn't by running straight for it and body-checking everyone else out of your way, but rather by becoming the least. "Whoever wishes to become great among you shall be your servant; and whoever wishes to be first among you shall be slave of all" (Mark 10:43-44).

You have to pursue greatness indirectly, through service, sacrifice, and self-denial, with eyes of faith fixed on God's promises and on that invisible, imperishable wreath. Don't focus on becoming some great person in the eyes of the world, but rather focus on becoming the least, "for everyone who exalts himself will be humbled, and he who humbles himself will be exalted" (Luke 14:11).

Serve others as if you were the least important of all (Matthew 20:26), knowing for certain that those who serve most will be most exalted. If you want to make a serious go at being the greatest in heaven, you've got to brush up on your sense of irony and ask your enemies if their toilets could use a good scrubbing. To become a king, you have to first become a servant, and to submit to the rocky seas of persecution:

> Who would not be willing to venture on the seas, though rough and tempestuous, if he was sure to be crowned as soon as he came ashore? Persecutors may take away from us our goods but not our God; our liberty but not our freedom of conscience; our head, but not our crown.[77]

You can't expect to become a king in Christ's kingdom apart from a crown of thorns. "For just as the sufferings of Christ are ours in abundance, so also our comfort is abundant through Christ" (2 Corinthians 1:5). Moses chose earthly suffering over all the riches and earthly pleasures of Egypt, because he looked past the immediate urges of his belly and set his eyes on the invisible, spiritual reward:

> By faith Moses, when he had grown up, refused to be called the son of Pharaoh's daughter, choosing rather to endure ill-treatment with the people of God than to enjoy the passing pleasures of sin, considering the reproach of Christ greater riches than the treasures of Egypt; for he was looking to the reward. By faith he left Egypt, not fearing the

---

[77] Watson, Self-Denial, 76%.

wrath of the king; for he endured, as seeing Him
who is unseen.

(Hebrews 11:24-27)

Moses understood, at some level, that the road paved with suffering
led to an unending world of pleasure and glory. He was able to see
his sacrifices as investments in himself. He was a forward-thinking
Christian Hedonist, and God the Holy Spirit, speaking in the pages
of Scripture, praises him for it. Moses understood that a persecuted
person with his heart in heaven is smiling and laughing all the way
to the bank. "Consider it all joy, my brethren, when you encounter
various trials" (James 1:2). Trials are temporary discomforts tending
unto eternal gain:

> The considerations of heaven and glory will make
> the believer submit to anything here. He can be
> content to be poor, for he knows he shall be rich; to
> be reproached, for he knows he shall be honoured;
> to be afflicted, for he knows he shall be comforted;
> to be imprisoned, for he knows he shall be brought
> into a large place....to lose all, for he knows he shall
> find all hereafter. God will be all, and more than all,
> to him. He knows that the trials last but for a little
> season, a day, an hour, a moment, a small moment.
> Hereafter there are eternal embraces.[78]

You should view yourself from God's eternal perspective, as
revealed to us in Scripture, and so see yourself as blessed in the face
of trial and persecution, for "when the heart is much in heaven, the
earth will seem a small thing,"[79] and it is but a small suffering for a
great reward. "For momentary, light affliction," said the Apostle, "is
producing for us an eternal weight of glory far beyond all
comparison, while we look not at the things which are seen, but at

---

[78] Bolton, Bounds, 91%.
[79] Manton, Self-Denial, 18%.

the things which are not seen; for the things which are seen are temporal, but the things which are not seen are eternal" (2 Corinthians 4:17-18). Paul went on to conclude, "therefore I take pleasure in infirmities, in reproaches, in necessities, in persecutions, in distresses for Christ's sake: for when I am weak, then am I strong." (2 Corinthians 12:10 KJV)

Nothing ever happens to us that can't be used for our own benefit. There is always a way of hedonistic escape. "Oh, what a good God do we serve, when we can even bless Him for afflictions! A Christian can sing in winter as well as in the spring."[80] Christian Hedonism views every relationship and every situation as a source of potential benefit to the self, and it should be clear at this point that Christian Hedonism is simply biblical Christianity as pertaining to the rational motivation to follow after Christ wholeheartedly. "Whatever you do, do your work heartily, as for the Lord rather than for men, knowing that from the Lord you will receive the reward of the inheritance" (Colossians 3:23-24). Put all men above yourself, as you would have them do unto you, that all alike may be lifted high above the world.

Let's recap where we've been so far. The question is not whether I should serve God *or* others *or* self, but rather, I should honor God by whole-heartedly seeking his rewards for myself in the service of others. Likewise, it's not a choice between seeking pleasure in this life *or* the next life, but rather seeking pleasure in this life *and* the next life by forsaking the life of sin and running hard after righteousness.

My overall argument, then, is that there is no downside whatsoever to the Christian life, provided the matter is judged rightly from a spiritual, biblical perspective. A Christian Hedonist gains everything at no cost to himself, for everything he loses is either not worth keeping, or else is more valuable to himself when given away.

---

[80] Manton, Self-Denial 54%.

THE DEVIL'S DISTRACTION

We have thus far spent a great deal of time noting the character of true self-denial and a wholesome, redeemed sense of self-interest. We have seen that these are not at all in conflict or contradiction to one another, for the thing denied and the thing sought after are not the same thing. We deny ourselves that which is harmful to us and pursue that which tends unto lasting satisfaction. We deny ourselves inferior treasures in order to gain superior treasures. Both our self-denial in sin and our self-affirmation in righteousness tend ultimately unto our best interest; in both cases, the Bible affirms that self-interest is a God-given blessing.

Here I hope to round out the entire discussion by attempting to demonstrate the absurdity and futility of that contrary view that says self-interest is of little to no value and should not be a consideration in our decision making. This will require a slightly deeper dive than we have taken thus far. However, if you agree with what has been said, by and large, and don't care to hear about the contrary view, you could skip to the next chapter without much harm.

Modern philosophers distinguish between two different views on the subject of self-interest. Those who affirm that self-interest has an appropriate place in ethics are called "egoists," while those who argue that self-interest should never be a consideration in ethics are called "altruists." Both groups of thinkers tend to have trouble with the issue of self-sacrifice. To put it simply, egoists struggle to justify sacrificing for others because they're in it for themselves, while altruists struggle to offer any coherent motivation or incentive to sacrifice, because the very idea of a personal incentive is self-interested. In both cases, self-sacrifice can seem very difficult to justify on a strictly rational basis.

Christian Hedonism is undoubtedly a form of egoism, yet its commitment to a consistently Christian, biblical point of view enables it to easily avoid the pitfalls of worldly philosophy. Not only do we find a rational justification for self-sacrifice, but we find rational justification for making self-sacrifice one of life's primary aims. In short, I should sacrifice my time, money, and energy for others because it's in my own long-term best interest, because God has promised me tremendous everlasting rewards for doing so and God is glorified when I seek his rewards. Not only that, but those who sacrifice for others in the name of Christ, who live their life for the sake of heaven, attain the greatest peace and satisfaction both at this time and in the age to come.

The term "egoism" is unfortunate; it sounds more like a serious character flaw than a formal philosophical position. Almost immediately we feel we have entered into the presence of egotistical, egocentric egomaniacs. It sounds like the sort of title you'd try to pin your enemy with, and, as a matter of fact, that's exactly how the term came about. The term "egoism" was coined by the French philosopher, Auguste Comte (1798-1857), a self-proclaimed altruist. This helps to explain why "altruism" has a much more pleasant, pious ring to it.

As Christians, we know we live in a world of spiritual conflict. The visible disputes of the political realm that sometimes boil over into military conflict are merely the visible outworkings of an intense, invisible, world-wide conflict. The men of this world often seem to look to politics for salvation, as if the next leader will be able to wipe the slate clean and turn everything around. Yet the same problems persist from leader to leader and generation to generation because those problems are merely the visible symptoms of a much deeper spiritual crisis. "Our struggle is not against flesh and blood, but against the rulers, against the powers, against the world forces of this darkness, against the spiritual forces of wickedness in the heavenly places" (Ephesians 6:12).

The forces of evil do not fight blindly in this war, but strategically and intelligently, as if for their very lives. Satan becomes the "god" of this world (2 Corinthians 4:4), gaining practical influence by eroding morality and promoting intellectual delusion. He procures his own advantage (or so he imagines) by doing everything he can to distract our eyes away from the eternal wreath by making sin appear as virtuous and as valuable as possible. Sometimes he even pretends to be a moralist. He disguises himself as a virtuous angel of light when it best suits his purposes (cf. 2 Corinthians 11:14). Where "altruism" sounds like a compliment or a great feat, I would liken this to a wolf in sheep's clothing.

Altruists believe we should live for others and not for self. Seeking a personal reward in a good deed is seen as tarnishing the quality of that good deed. A truly moral deed should spring spontaneously from one's highest sense of duty unto others and should be indifferent to personal gain, personal inclinations, or personal consequences. Immanuel Kant (1724-1804), the German idealist philosopher, argued, for example, that there is "no true moral worth" in having a natural inclination or disposition toward kind deeds, for the kind deeds have become self-serving in that case.[81]

Superficially that sounds commendable, perhaps even praiseworthy, but consider what is actually being said: you should

---

[81] In the *Foundations of the Metaphysics of Morals* he writes, "To be kind where one can is a duty, and there are, moreover, many persons so sympathetically constituted that without any motive of vanity or selfishness they find an inner satisfaction in spreading joy and rejoicing in the contentment of others which they have made possible. But I say that, however dutiful and however amiable it may be, that kind of action has no true moral worth... For the maxim lacks the moral import of an action done not from inclination but from duty." Section 1.397-399, quoted in Rogers, Anthology, 162-163.

never seek to *enjoy* morality or *benefit from* morality, for then you'd personally be gaining something from it, and then it would cease to be morality. Notice what has happened in the altruist scheme. Satan has introduced confusion by blurring the line between self-interest and selfishness. The suggestion is subtly raised that seeking anything good for yourself through your good deeds is inherently selfish. Morality is defined as disinterested, emotionless duty. Practically speaking, morality and pleasure are defined as polar opposites. The logic the Devil wants to sell you is that morality is only really morality when you get nothing out of it and hate every minute of it. Doing good deeds on account of heavenly treasure becomes a criminal offense.

Satan introduces confusion and distraction by drawing our eyes away from God's rewards and unto smug, barren, worldly notions. Here "duty" is not duty unto our Creator, but "duty" unto my own sense of self-righteousness, "duty" thrown into the void of empty ideals. Here "indifference" is not turning your back on sin, but rather turning your back on the Creator's promises and rewards. Here "morality" is not the Holy Spirit working in the heart to bring about repentance, but rather the spontaneous, irrational stirring of yourself, by yourself, to deeds that gain nothing for yourself. Even though God himself cannot sin (cf. 1 John 3:9) and always has a natural inclination to do good, the Altruist warns us not to have such an inclination. Kant warns us that—whatever we do—we should never hunger or thirst for righteousness, for then it would cease to be righteousness.

If you think back to the gloomy face of the fasting Pharisee, you will remember that wickedness often conceals itself behind a veil of piety. Altruism undoubtedly has a semblance of virtue, but it's only a semblance. It's like the whitewashed tomb that appears pure on the outside but is full of maggots and rottenness on the inside. The Altruist says we should not seek rewards for ourselves in our good deeds, yet according to Geerhardus Vos (1862-1949), the great Dutch theologian, this view is idolatry on a number of levels:

> In order to reach clearness on the question [of the appropriateness of seeking rewards] we must first disabuse ourselves of the modern idea as though every thought of reward in ethical relations were unworthy of the sacredness of ethics. This is an opinion ultimately based on the philosophy of the autonomy or deification of ethics, and behind that on the principle of unmotived free will. Man is not such an autonomous being that he can afford to scorn a reward from God, provided the idea of meritoriousness be kept absent from it. If that were man's normal ethical attitude, then man would be in ethics like unto God. Of Jesus Himself it is said that the idea of reward attracted and sustained Him and determined the result of His work (Heb 12:2).[82]

When we define morality as the opposite of pleasure-seeking, we've all but conceded that the life of sin is where all the real pleasure is. Likewise, when we define self-seeking as inherently immoral, we automatically define immorality as the best way to be self-seeking. I disagree with a great deal of Ayn Rand's atheistic philosophy, but here she struck upon a very profound and important truth:

> [In learning that self-interest is evil] the first thing [a person] learns is that morality is his enemy: he has nothing to gain from it, he can only lose; self-inflicted loss, self-inflicted pain and the gray, debilitating pall of an incomprehensible duty is all that he can expect. He may hope that others might

---

[82] Vos, Biblical, 394-395.

occasionally sacrifice themselves for his benefit, as he grudgingly sacrifices himself for theirs, but he knows that the relationship will bring mutual resentment, not pleasure—and that, morally, their pursuit of values will be like an exchange of unwanted, unchosen Christmas presents, which neither is morally permitted to buy for himself. Apart from such times as he manages to perform some act of self-sacrifice, he possesses no moral significance: morality takes no cognizance of him and has nothing to say to him for guidance in the crucial issues of his life; it is only his own personal, private, "selfish" life... [which gives him guidance, though] it is regarded... as evil...[83]

The devil's best method of promoting immorality is simply by convincing us that morality has nothing to offer. He need not persuade us to be openly immoral, when persuading us to pursue a disinterested morality will be just as effective at making us disinterested in morality. When we define morality as the opposite of self-seeking, then, practically speaking, we define morality as useless to the self-seeking. Goodness is subtly, inadvertently defined as the "non-good for me."[84]

Altruists believe an action is only truly moral if it is done without regard for our own interests or rewards. Any action which looks toward personal gain is automatically deemed to be immoral. This raises the question, however, what could possibly be the altruist's motivation? If he manages to find some personal incentive to sacrifice for another, then he has defeated his own position. In its very conception, altruism excludes the possibility of ever having any personal *reason* to sacrifice for another. The altruist believes he must sacrifice without any personal motivation for doing so, yet the

---

[83] Rand, Virtue, viii.
[84] Rand, Atlas Shrugged, quoted in Rogers, Anthology, 245.

very idea of an *unmotivated* action is nonsense from a rational standpoint, an effect without a cause. Every human action has a motive, and every human motive has some human *urge* behind it.

The Devil need not persuade us to carry the banner of gross immorality above our heads when the banner of a false humility will do just as well.[85] The man who sacrifices of himself while refusing to find any external motivation in God and God's rewards will inevitably be tricked into searching for a personal motivation in his own pride. If you're not sacrificing for the reward from God, you'll inevitably begin harboring the secret motivation of thinking highly of yourself for being so selfless. You'll think well of yourself for being too "noble" to seek after personal gain in your good deeds. In this though, an altruist has again betrayed his own position, for pride itself has become his personal incentive. All roads lead inevitably back to self-interest; no one ever hated their own flesh.

Only God himself is self-sustaining, yet the altruist imagines himself to be self-sustaining when he imagines himself being moral apart from any and every external benefit. He'll inevitably think highly of himself for disregarding himself. Frederich Nietzsche (1844-1900), the infamous atheist, noted that, in many cases, "he who despises himself feels at the same time respect for himself as a despiser."[86] False humility is imagining yourself to be the kind of person who is self-motivated and sufficient in your own strength to do the right thing, while true humility is embracing God as the source of all pure motivation and the rewarder of those who seek him.

> "False humility says, 'I want no reward.' Effectively that means, 'I want nothing to lay at Christ's feet to bring him glory.' We may think we are taking the spiritual high ground by being disinterested in

---

85 It probably goes without saying that the chapter owes something to old Screwtape.
86 Nietzsche, Beyond Good and Evil, quoted in Nygren, Agape, 121.

rewards, but this is foreign to Scripture. Of course we should desire rewards. Hearing our Master say, 'Well done' will not simply be for our pleasure but for his!"[87]

This cuts to the very core of Christian motivation. The great danger of the altruistic idea that *it's not about me* is that it's but a hair's breadth from *it doesn't interest me, because there's nothing in it for me.* All that message ever does—all it has ever done—is sap our motivation. Personal incentive is ruled out right at the starting line; there is no laurel wreath to run for, and even if there was a wreath, it would be wrong to run for it.

Satan wants nothing more than to distract our eyes from the eternal wreath, and his very best trick to date has been to convince us that it's wrong to desire eternal wreaths for ourselves. Pastors and priests across the globe shout from their pulpits that "it's not about you!" and that you should stop desiring so much good for yourself, but this is a lie! Sam Storms, the contemporary American pastor and author, rightly noted,

> One of the worst injustices the church has perpetrated against its members is proclaiming a message of the evil of desire. God created us with a longing to be thrilled, hungry for the joy of being fascinated. Yet we have told people to stop wanting and to stop yearning; we've urged them to ignore, suppress, or anesthetize their desire for happiness...All this will do is drive passion underground...only to have it erupt at some moment

---

[87] Alcorn, Rewards, 92.

of weakness when temptation offers a fleeting fulfillment.[88]

Seeing sacrifice as staking your claim in the infinite riches of the Father will give you real personal motivation to sacrifice, whereas if you feel morally obligated to never pursue your own good then you have no choice but to believe it's inherently wrong to look toward spiritual rewards. This cannot possibly produce anything beyond a begrudging duty, yet God does not delight in those who are only willing to serve him begrudgingly (cf. Deuteronomy 28:47-48). "The obedience of dutiful drudgery is better, but only marginally so, than outright disobedience."[89]

At a practical level, the altruist is obligated to count his good deeds as a total loss to himself. If he's personally seeking to get something out of it, then it's not a good deed at all. Yet who is more likely to *actually* sacrifice? The man with personal motivation to sacrifice or the man with no personal motivation? The man with incentive or the man with no incentive? How likely is it you'll be excited to sacrifice for the good of another, when you are forced to account that sacrifice a personal loss? That sort of sacrifice would be nothing short of hating your own flesh.

It is indeed a profound injustice that so many people have been trained by their church leaders (oftentimes in very subtle, vague, semi-conscious ways) that they should smash their own Christian joy every time it creeps back into their heart. They tell themselves God must not be enjoyed but rather served out of a disinterested and selfless sense of duty. Yet this is nothing but a lie of the devil, who will do anything he can to keep us from being satisfied with God or truly motivated to serve God. Satan wants us to be sluggish and slothful in pursuing rewards. He wants us to believe it's wrong to seek a God who rewards, because when we don't seek a God who rewards, then we don't seek the true God at

---

88 Storms, Evermore, 43.
89 Alcorn, Happiness, 414.

all, but merely some figment of the pagan imagination. That old snake must thoroughly enjoy watching us tell ourselves the right and moral thing to do is to follow God in a selfless and disinterested way, with no real personal interest or stake in God, when this is the very definition of hypocrisy!

It is telling that many Christian scholars during the Middle Ages argued that we should harbor a sense of complete "apathy."[90] The general intention of this expression was to indicate that we should be unmoved in the face of trials. We shouldn't be driven by sinful passions and fickle emotions. Fair enough, yet all too often it proved to be a slippery slope that quickly decayed into the altruistic notion that personal incentives shouldn't motivate our action, and that we should be apathetic toward our own personal gain.

The glorification of a Stoic sense of indifference can easily leave the impression that what God really wants is for us not to desire anything for ourselves (including even God himself). The rulers of the darkness of this world have all but won when Christians preach a gospel of apathy and indifference. These are horrific crimes masquerading as virtues.

The Devil would have us believe that if we give everything for the sake of the heavenly reward, we haven't really given anything at all. In truth, however, it's only when you give everything for the sake of the reward from God that you've truly given everything to God, because you've then forsaken every motivation outside of God. Only when you seek the reward from the hand of God have you truly forsaken this world's empty promises.

Even where it presents itself as Christian,[91] altruism is not a Christian notion, but a pagan one:

---

[90] See the discussion in Nygren, Agape, 596-597 and following.

[91] A good practical example of Christian Altruism can be found in Jay Adams' *The Biblical View of Self-Esteem, Self-Love, Self-Image*. A good academic example can be found in Anders Nygren's *Agape and Eros*. Neither author uses the term "altruism" but the basic outlook of an absolute self-denial is clear enough. Both authors appeal more to intuition than to the Bible or actual argumentation.

I wonder what forethought a person has of heaven and what he thinks of glory and salvation, when he says that we are not to eye these [rewards], nor to have respect to them in our obedience. Certainly he thinks of them under false notions. His thoughts are not God's thoughts. He looks upon them as the world does, carnally, not spiritually. None will own that heaven as his happiness which he may not have respect to in his service; nay, which he does not make his ambition and his aim in his service.[92]

If you consider it carefully, you'll see that all the major doctrines of the Christian faith necessitate self-interest. If it's wrong to seek your own good, then isn't it also wrong to believe in heaven? For isn't heaven, by definition, a place of personal satisfaction? If self-interest and morality are opposed to one another, wouldn't it be wrong for God to tempt us with the personal satisfaction of heaven? Even faith itself stands upon the foundation of self-interest. To be saved, you must see the prospect of salvation as a benefit to yourself. You must recognize yourself as trapped in a sorry state and needful of a personal deliverance from a personal Savior. On this point, the Roman Catholic, Greek Orthodox, and Protestant Evangelical are all in agreement. Wherever Christ is proclaimed, he is proclaimed as a personal blessing, and so it will be until the end of the age, and, indeed, for all eternity.

Not only is it *not* a sin to seek your own good, it's an absolute moral obligation. You must lay up treasure in heaven! You must love others as you love yourself! You must seek satisfaction in hungering and thirsting for righteousness! So often we dismiss these blessed commandments as being somehow insincere. We smile and nod and tell ourselves we agree, when in fact, in our heart of hearts, we've immediately written them off as not *really* meaning what they

---

Kierkegaard (a Lutheran) also tends toward Altruism in *Works of Love*, but rarely seems concerned with consistency.
[92] (Bolton, Bounds, 88%).

seem at first to mean. Oh friends, I am fearful that we're so backwards in our thinking—so messed up in the head—that sometimes we dismiss the very commandments of God as selfish immorality!

Trying to rid yourself of self-interest is a stupid, worldly idea that must be forsaken. It is contrary to God's design, impossible to practice with any degree of consistency. Altruism betrays itself as superficial and hypocritical at every stage. Kant could only lament that "the dear self" is always getting in the way of selfless duty, and that it is, therefore, "sometimes doubtful whether true virtue can really be found anywhere in the world."[93]

I know what I'm saying is counter-intuitive in some ways. I know it seems to cut against the grain of common sense in some ways. Yet that's because our intuition itself is in need of renewal. It's no easy endeavor, but we have to learn to trust the Word of God more than we trust our own intuition. What we find in the Bible is that God wants us to run hard for the prize and to see that prize as valuable for ourselves. The real goal of the Christian life is not to try to turn off desire, but rather to focus it on the right objects, and then to turn it up all the way. Augustine said it best: "Conduct the water which is flowing into the sewer, to the garden instead. Such a strong urge as it had to the world, let it have to the Creator of the world."[94]

---

[93] Quoted in Rogers, Anthology, 164.
[94] Augustine, Exposition of the Psalms, quoted in Nygren, Agape, 735.

GOD'S LOVE OF SELF

We have made every effort thus far to think seriously about the blessings God bestows on us, both in terms of rewards in heaven and spiritual satisfaction on earth. Though such topics are worthy of much consideration, still our project has been somewhat one-sided up to this point. To put it simply, we've talked a lot about what's in it for us, but have said very little about what (if anything) is in it for God.

Such a topic may seem overly abstract and perhaps not very practical, but remember, we're doing what we can to open our Bibles and to think God's thoughts after him so as to gain some perspective on ourselves. That being the case, if we were to exclude the consideration of God himself in our effort to think God's thoughts after him, our task would seem highly superficial, if not downright hypocritical. *Knowing God* finds favor in the sight of God (Exodus 33:13), and we cannot hope to gain any real perspective on ourselves without trying to gain some perspective on our Creator.

Far from being impractical, I believe the pages ahead of us have more power to change our lives than the pages left behind, so I urge you to press on. I'm completely convinced that a little bit of knowledge about who God is will do you more good than a whole truckload of Christian self-help books. If you want to be filled, don't be content with theological appetizers, but rather order the steak, and do what you can to finish the whole thing (cf. 1 Corinthians 3:2). One possible place to start is the next paragraph.

We should first note that God's personal motivations for creating the world have not been kept a secret from us in the least. The Bible states very plainly, in straight-forward terms, literally hundreds of times, that God created all things for his own glory:

> Thou art worthy, O Lord, to receive glory and
> honour and power: for thou hast created all things,
> and for thy pleasure they are and were created.
>
> *(Revelation 4:11 KJV)*

God created the world for his own ends, namely, his own glory, honor, and pleasure. Everything in the world was created by the Father through the Son and exists ultimately for God's own purposes; "all things were created by him, and *for him*" (Colossians 1:16). When God exiled many of the Jews to Babylon on account of their unfaithfulness, he was also quick to encourage them that he would bring them home again soon. Notice his purpose in it:

> "Do not fear, for I am with you;
> I will bring your offspring from the east,
> And gather you from the west.
> "I will say to the north, 'Give them up!'
> And to the south, 'Do not hold them back.'
> Bring My sons from afar
> And My daughters from the ends of the earth,
> Everyone who is called by My name,
> And whom I have created for My glory,
> Whom I have formed, even whom I have made."
>
> *(Isaiah 43:5-7)*

Their trials in exile were, at least in part, to test them to see what was in them, so that those who were true to him would have the opportunity to lay up great rewards, and those who were not true to him would be revealed as imposters and invited to repent. Curiously enough, even God's astonishing patience and mercy to us is, ultimately, for his own benefit, unto the praise of his own name:

> "For the sake of My name I delay My wrath,
> And for My praise I restrain it for you,
> In order not to cut you off.
> "Behold, I have refined you, but not as silver;
> I have tested you in the furnace of affliction.
> "For My own sake, for My own sake, I will act;
> For how can My name be profaned?
> And My glory I will not give to another.
>
> *(Isaiah 48:9-11)*

The ultimate purpose of God's creation is to promote God's glory; this is the purpose he had in view from the beginning. This is the most basic reason why the world exists. God called Israel for his glory (cf. Isaiah 49:3, Jeremiah 13:11). He redeemed Israel from Egypt for his glory (cf. Psalm 106:8). He raised up Pharaoh for his glory (cf. Romans 9:17). He defeated Pharaoh for his glory (cf. Exodus 14:18). He spared Israel in the wilderness for his glory (cf. Ezekiel 20:14). He drove out the Canaanites for his glory (cf. 2 Samuel 7:23). He defended and preserved Jerusalem for a long time for his glory (cf. 2 Kings 19:34). He restored his people from exile for his glory (cf. Ezekiel 36:22-23).

All men stand before him condemned by nature, because they have fallen short of his glory (cf. Romans 9:22-23) and traded away his glory on account of their sin (cf. Romans 1:22-23), but he forgives the sins of the repentant for the sake of his glory (cf. Isaiah 43:25, Psalm 25:11, Isaiah 43:25). Everything he does, he does for his own purpose, and all unto his own glory (cf. Ephesians 1:11-12). Even those who hate him still glorify him, despite themselves (cf. Psalm 76:10, Proverbs 16:4). Just as God is, forever and always, unchangingly God, so too he is unchangingly interested, first and foremost, in God. "He's a hedonist at heart."[95]

These truths about God's motivation for creating the world often strike people as selfish, but this is based, in no small measure, on a faulty understanding of self-interest. As we have been saying all along, it is quite commonly imagined that people are supposed to turn off their sense of self-interest, such that a perfectly ethical person would no longer care about themselves and only act in the interest of others. Complete self-disregard is regarded as man's highest ethical aim, and he quickly applies this standard to God as well. The old man believes God should not be concerned about God, but should rather concern himself exclusively with man's pleasure and glory.

As a result of Adam's sin, man is fallen by nature. All of human life is warped by sin, even man's mind and intellectual life (cf. Titus 1:15). We each begin our journey through life with a backwards, broken philosophy. We set out on the wrong footing, heading down the wrong path, and very few ever find their way back (cf. Matthew 7:13-14). When the Apostle Paul refers to the "elementary principles of the world" (Colossians 2:8), he seems to be referring, at least in part, to the faulty patterns of thinking shared by all fallen men. The notion that self-interest is somehow inherently evil is undoubtedly near the top of the list of the world's "elementary principles." This faulty point of view is not limited to the modern era, but can be seen in the records of every age.

Here's how I suspect this faulty assumption comes about. From the very time we begin to think and act, we naturally, instinctively pursue our own good. There's nothing wrong with this desire to pursue our own good, but unfortunately, because of our fallen nature, we pursue our own good through a sinful, shortcut, smash-and-grab approach. As a result of our sin, our God-given conscience is afflicted. In this, our conscience has a settled stability and resolve that we ourselves do not have; it stands before us as a judge accusing us of our wrongdoing. We have to make excuses to

---

[95] Lewis, Screwtape, 249.

ourselves. We have to shift the blame away from ourselves. We have to try to justify ourselves *to ourselves* (cf. Romans 2:15). We wish we could turn off this innate sense of right and wrong so as to enjoy our sin without the disruption of guilt. We come to hate our own God-given conscience, and thus become enemies of ourselves, set on our own self-destruction. The worst thing that can happen to us is God giving us what we want and letting us go our own way (cf. Romans 1:24). God is exceedingly patient with us though, and his patience is designed to lead us to repentance (Romans 2:4), for he does not delight in the death of the wicked (Ezekiel 33:11). God openly and sincerely invites all men to come to him, and he never restrains anyone from coming to him.

In this way, the old man feels that his own tastes and interests run contrary to the interests of his own conscience. He is at war with himself, divided and conflicted against himself. At the same time, the outside world shouts at him—clearly, loudly, frequently—that he must stop thinking about himself so much. Everyone he encounters seems in agreement that whatever he is to be, he must certainly not be selfish. In most cases, this is little more than a manipulation tactic; we typically call someone "selfish" because they're not doing what we would (selfishly) prefer them to do for us. The old man thus feels that both the world and his own conscience are against him—against his *self* and against his *interests*—and thus seem in agreement that the problem lies somehow in his self-interest.

In accepting the world's great lie that self-interest is evil, the sinner overlooks the real problem entirely. The real problem is not his self-interest, but rather the *sinful objects* his self-interest is directed towards. As Edwards noted, "The error is not so much in the degree of his love to himself as it is in the channel in which it flows. It is not in the degree in which he loves his own happiness, but in his placing his happiness where he ought not, and in limiting and confining his love."[96] The old man's problem is not that he seeks happiness for himself, but that he seeks it in the sewer.

Fallen man feels a constant tension between doing *the right thing* and doing *what he wants to do*, and he makes the mistake of thinking the problem is doing *what he wants to do*, when the real problem is that what he wants to do is sin. The self which feels it must be selfless and against itself is a self with a wounded and guilty conscience, bound under a law of sin (cf. Romans 6:12-14). The old man understands, at some level, that his particular variety of self-interest is sinful, and he wrongly infers from this that all self-interest is sinful.

As we have said, man is hard-wired to seek his own good, and thus he cannot but seek his own good. While redeemed man and fallen man each equally seek their own good, fallen man, in his profound confusion, seeks his good in contradiction to the design of his Creator, and thus dishonors both God and himself. He robs God of his glory just as surely as he robs himself of true joy and pleasure. What is worse is that fallen man assumes God should support him in this endeavor because he thinks God should live up to his highest ethical ideals, including the denial of one's own self-interest. He thinks God should forgo his own desires and kneel to the wishes and whims of sinful man. C.S. Lewis put it very practically when he said:

> What would really satisfy us would be a God who said of anything we happened to like doing, 'What does it matter so long as they are contented?' We want, in fact, not so much a Father in Heaven as a grandfather in heaven—a senile benevolence who, as they say, 'liked to see young people enjoying themselves' and whose plan for the universe was simply that it might be truly said at the end of each

---

[96] Edwards, Charity, 164.

day, 'a good time was had by all'.[97]

What would really satisfy us is a God who thinks our thoughts after us. Take, for example, the single most common argument against the existence of God today, the so-called "problem of evil." It runs as follows: if God were both good and powerful, as Christians affirm him to be, evil would not exist, because God would surely wipe it out. Since evil exists, presumably either God does not exist, or else he is not powerful enough or good enough to wipe it out. Though the form of the argument may seem compelling at first, a few moments of serious consideration will show that there is not ultimately any real substance to it. We can easily see at this point that, foremost among its many faulty "elementary principles" is the assumption that God has some unspoken obligation to be self-denying. It seems very plain, in other words, that there is an underlying assumption that God is somehow *obligated* to pursue man's pleasure more than he pursues his own. A good and powerful God, it is argued, *must* end all human suffering immediately.

Yet what if pain serves a greater purpose? What if pain was merely a means unto some greater end? After all, the Bible frequently attests that God uses pain to draw us unto himself. The suffering of a bad man is intended to draw him to repentance, for it would be a great disservice if God should let him rest content while travelling the wide road leading to destruction. His pain warns him of his mortality and the fleeting futility of his earthly treasures:

> We can rest contentedly in our sins and in our stupidities...But pain insists upon being attended to. God whispers to us in our pleasures, speaks in our conscience, but shouts in our pain; it is His megaphone to rouse a deaf world.[98]

---

[97] Lewis, Pain, 569.
[98] Lewis, Pain, 604.

God is neither the author of evil nor suffering, for man corrupted himself of his own will. "Behold, I have found only this, that God made men upright, but they have sought out many devices" (Ecclesiastes 7:29). Nevertheless, in his vast mercy, God continues to shower blessings on all men (Matthew 5:45). "If we are faithless, He remains faithful, for He cannot deny Himself" (2 Timothy 2:13). He hears all who cry out to him in sincerity and does not delay in offering them aid (Psalm 22:24). God takes no joy in suffering, and suffering is never an end in itself (cf. Lamentations 3:33), but even suffering is a kindness of God, for it is intended to promote human repentance (cf. Romans 2:4).

By and large, pain is an unusual state. In pain, we are reminded of the countless blessings God has given us at all other times in our life. We are reminded of how little we have acknowledged all of the normal comforts God has continually showered upon us. We are called to consider both God's patience and our ungratefulness. In countless ways, God turns our suffering to our advantage and uses temporary pains to promote long-term advantage.

At the same time, God would be *less God* if he existed simply to cater to the whims of sinners. Ancient Christian thinkers were fond of saying it is natural that a lesser honors a greater. Men have seeing-eye dogs, but dogs don't have seeing-eye men. Subjects serve kings, employees serve employers, children obey parents; nature dictates that every creature owes honor to those in positions of authority over them (cf. Ephesians 6). Even God himself has a certain moral obligation (to himself) to honor the greater over the lesser, but, as he looks about him, he sees *no other*. He casts his gaze infinitely in every direction and sees that there is none more honorable than himself, and so he rightly, righteously reserves the greatest portion for himself. If God were to value something more than God, then God would be replacing the greatest value for a lesser value, but that would be idolatry. As John Piper has noted:

We would not want an unrighteous God who valued anything more than what is most valuable—who tried to trick the market by bidding on silver when he knew all along that gold is best.[99]

"Perfect justice," said Augustine, is "to love the greater objects more and the lesser less."[100] Accordingly, God's goal in everything he does is to demonstrate love to God by glorifying God:

> Redemption, salvation, and restoration are not God's ultimate goal. These He performs for the sake of something greater: namely, the enjoyment He has in glorifying Himself. The bedrock foundation of Christian Hedonism is not God's allegiance to us, but to Himself.[101]

If God uses my pain for his ultimate glory, this would not be an injustice, but rather perfect justice, for God's highest moral obligation is not unto man, but unto God. Furthermore, if God simultaneously managed to use my pain for *my* ultimate glory as well, what then of the so-called problem of evil? It would not be a problem so much as an occasion for praise.

We need only to fix our eyes upon the cross to see the heart of God in the matter of suffering. God knows how to turn the most desperate of situations unto the happiest of ends. In the cross, we do not find suffering for the sake of suffering, but rather suffering for the sake of redemption and glory, that is, suffering for the sake of greater pleasure.

---

[99] Piper, Pleasures, 193.
[100] The True Religion, quoted in O'Donovan, Problem, 97.
[101] Piper, Desiring, 31.

THE GREAT DILEMMA

The reason man is self-interested and cannot be otherwise is because man was created by God who is self-interested and cannot be otherwise. God can no sooner turn off his unshakeable sense of self-interest than you or I can, yet this seems to bring us upon a great dilemma, since these two self-interests may seem, at first glance, to contradict one another and to head, as it were, in opposite directions. If God cannot *but* be self-interested, and man cannot *but* be self-interested, would not God and man be forever locked in conflict? Wouldn't man's interests ultimately be forced to lose out to God's interests?

Let's put the dilemma in the strongest terms we can before we look for a solution. On the one hand, God is the highest being and the being for which all other beings were created, and so it seems necessary and natural that God be exalted highest in every individual consciousness, exactly as we've been saying. Even the demons and the damned are still under the absolute moral obligation to praise, honor, and glorify God as the most valuable, most praise-worthy being, though, in their complete moral blindness, they refuse to acknowledge it.

On the other hand, however, all of my actions begin ultimately *with me* and must center upon my own perception of where my own good lies. I simply cannot hate my own flesh, or turn off my own self-interest, and my will and affections have their initial starting point, in every instance, *in myself*.

In short, God demands honor and glory yet I demand happiness and satisfaction, and neither of us can turn off this desire for our own good, so how can these two ever be reconciled?

Now, I do believe there is a short and straight-forward answer to the question. We have, no doubt, hinted at it many times already. I'm confident that we'll discover a happy resolution momentarily, but if you'll bear with me a moment, I'd like to take a more scenic, roundabout path. I beg you for your patience, for this is about as roundabout as it gets.

I'm a big fireworks fan. I really like them. I also hate fireworks because they're a tremendous waste of money. They're about as poor an investment as you can make really. From a financial perspective, it's really only one step removed from lighting your cash on fire to see the sizzle. I still buy some every year though; I can hardly help myself.

I like the crazy, colorful boxes they come in, marked up and down with explosive images, bold colors, and mysterious Chinese characters. I like the sense of mystery as to what they might do. There's generally a description of what they do on the side of the box there, but it's always too vague to be of any real use (both the big ones and the little ones all seem to say "shoots flaming balls and reports" which makes me think of high school book reports flying through the air on fire). I like how alien fireworks feel. The names aren't household names, the boxes are all very unique and unfamiliar, and what's inside could seemingly range from total dud to disastrously life-changing to totally epic and anything in between.

The shopping is fun, but the best part, of course, is the show itself. There's a little bit of danger, and a little bit of intrigue, and that delightful smell, something like a battlefield giving birth to a cigar shop. Most of all, I like that I can't quite wrap my mind around what I'm witnessing. In an instant, a lit fuse starts a chain reaction in which a billion particles of chemically colored gunpowder burst into shape and color overhead, and the awesome thunder of it echoes for miles. The whole thing is delightfully overwhelming. There's really too much to take in at once, so I find myself never being able to decide whether to focus on the left side, the right side, the top, the bottom, or to try to let my eyes blur a little so as to try to take in the whole scene at once. I like that fireworks are incomprehensible in some ways, unfathomable in some ways, indescribable in some ways, overwhelming in some ways.

You see, man was designed to wonder. We bite into a cupcake and as the sugary goodness melts across some 10,000 taste buds, we close our eyes in ecstasy, as if to live in that little world behind our teeth for a moment, as if that little world were sufficient and would be too much in conjunction with the world of sight.

We stand before the band as the guitar and the bass and the drums and the vocals all come together in harmony and melody and rhythm, alternating between verse and chorus, tension and release, overwhelming us in a complex, audible feast.

We stand on the precipice at sunset, the breeze and the rays dancing across some hundred billion nerves in our skin, as the countless miles of lakes and mountaintops steal our breath away and make us feel significant and strangely insignificant all at once.

We wonder at unbelievable slam dunks, and terrific amounts of horsepower, and million-dollar views, and romantic spectacles, and our new personal best in the marathon or the bench press or the video game or the salary—and those are all good things, but they're not the end for which you were created. You shouldn't make those things your god by giving them the highest practical place in your life, pouring all of your time, money, and energy into them.

Man was designed to wonder and nothing can be more cause for wonder than that which is most wonderful. The eyes of children always light up with wonder, because everything is new and the world is so big and completely wide-open. The child has not yet fully made sense of the world's mysteries; sensory delights outpace comprehension, filling him with awe and intrigue at every turn. In heaven that sense of wonder will never fade in the least for any of us, because the deeper our love and knowledge of God grows, the more we'll understand that we've only begun to scratch the surface of infinity. Century after century, age after age, we will feast upon the fireworks of God's glory, and yet always conclude, with Job, "Behold, these are the fringes of His ways; And how faint a word we hear of Him! But His mighty thunder, who can understand?" (26:14).

When you stand before your Maker in the sunshine of his being and every unfulfilled longing and unmet urge is entirely satisfied, and that in a myriad of ways you never anticipated, to heights and extents you never conceived of, nothing will ever have seemed so entirely natural to you as to worship the Lord of Glory. You will worship and glorify him for the pleasure you derive from worshipping and glorifying him in an endless, ecstatic loop, like a hedonistic GIF.

Nothing can satisfy a soul more than the end for which it was created, and you and I were designed to worship. You were made by God to worship and glorify God, and nothing can satisfy you like worshipping and glorifying God. You will see the dilemma entirely resolved in an instant when you come to understand that "the chief end of man is to glorify God by enjoying him forever."[102] You will find your greatest pleasure in the pursuit of his pleasure, and your greatest glory in the pursuit of his glory.

Just as the Hebrew Temple was an image or replica or earthly approximation of God's heavenly dwelling (Exodus 25:40, Ezekiel 43, Hebrews 8:5), so too our Sunday church service is an image of that future heavenly worship. We gather together each Lord's Day to rest from our earthly labors, to break bread, and to be warmed by the fruit of the vine and laughter and fellowship. We gather together to celebrate heaven early with the people of God and to sing the high praises of the Most High. Here we all seem to sing merely at the front wall, awkwardly and half-heartedly, missing

---

[102] https://www.desiringgod.org/messages/our-grand-obligation

the mark most of the time, but there the wall will be ripped away, exposing the glorious, earth-shaking reality.

In heaven, all the world's talent and energy and love will converge into the spotless and unveiled worship of the King, the train of whose robe fills the whole sanctuary (Isaiah 6:4). A trillion strings and a million drums and all the voices of the centuries will produce a symphony such as the world never imagined. In that world without end, we will sing unto the one whose voice shakes the foundations of the whole place (Isaiah 6:4), whose throne is surrounded by a glorious rainbow (Revelation 4:3).

Everything awkward and painful will have passed away, and we will sing and laugh and cry and dance together without restraint or even the tiniest inkling of fear or reservation. Here we see a few flickers of him, as through a dim textured glass (cf. 1 Corinthians 13:12), but there we will see him face to face in all his unveiled majesty and splendor. Here our interests are divided, but there everything will be harmony. "In this world, while we are here below, there is a great controversy between God and self; but in heaven the quarrel will be resolved, and we and God will be united in the nearest and closest way of union and communion, so that we may enjoy Him forever."[103]

God made man to worship himself, but being both good and wise, God made man to delight *in* worship. God has no interest in servile and forced worship. Rather he sought happy and willing worshippers and so designed man such that man is personally delighted by worship; indeed, delighted more in worship than in anything else.

God does not command us to include others in our self-love only to then turn around and love himself to the exclusion or detriment of others. Rather, he demonstrates his goodness to all men by showering blessings on all men (cf. Matthew 5:45). His mercies are everywhere present (Psalm 145:8-9). His arms are wide open to all who will come.

---

[103] Manton, Self-Denial, 74%.

John Piper summarized this blessed truth best: "God is most glorified in us when we are most satisfied in him."[104] In calling me to sing his praises, God is simultaneously calling me to pursue my own greatest pleasure. "In commanding us to glorify Him, God is inviting us to enjoy Him."[105] Denying God his right to pursue his own glorification to the fullest extent possible is, at the same time, denying man his right to pursue his own highest source of pleasure. If God is not to be fully glorified, then neither can I be fully satisfied. "When God is made ours, we love ourselves in loving God,"[106] because we recognize that our own good is found in his good.

Once again, the question is not my self-interest *or* God's self-interest, but rather we worship him for the euphoric pleasure the worship of him brings to the core of our very own beings. The biblical paradigm is my self-interest *through* God's self-interest, my joy through his worship. "The aim of God in all He does is His delight in our delight in Him."[107] God desires to be honored and worshipped, and honoring and worshipping God will bring a sort of satisfaction that will never begin to grow old and of which we will never tire. If such a vision strikes you as unfulfilling, pray to God that he would give you the spiritual eyes to catch a glimpse of the glorious reality that lies beyond the front wall of the church sanctuary.

God has made our happiness and pleasure in worship instrumental unto our craving and desire to worship him, and it is a complete waste of time to try to *not* enjoy it:

> The person who has the vague notion that it is virtue to overcome self-interest, and that it is vice to seek pleasure, will scarcely be able to worship. For worship is the most hedonistic affair of life and

---

104 Piper, Pleasures, 209.
105 Lewis, Psalms, 56%.
106 Manton, Self-Denial, 73%.
107 Storms, Evermore, 100.

must not be ruined with the least thought of disinterestedness. The great hindrance to worship is not that we are a pleasure-seeking people, but that we are willing to settle for such pitiful pleasures."[108]

My happiness in worship is the means God uses to secure a whole-hearted and sincere worship for himself. My satisfaction in worship is his incentive to me to worship. "The Bible does not force us to choose between God's glory and our joy. In fact, it forbids us to choose."[109] It's only when we see our greatest good in God that we can really pursue God wholly, without second-guessing whether our sacrifices were worth it or not. It's only after we've discovered that the Christian life is, in every way, the greatest of personal blessings that we really begin to pursue it with all our strength.

When we pray to God for our everyday needs and desires, we honor him by recognizing his power, sufficiency, and ability to accomplish all we ask in faith. When he answers our prayer (in his timing and his way), we honor him by expressing thanksgiving to him for his blessings unto us. It is his glory to be asked and also his glory to answer. Listen to what he said to the Psalmist: "Call upon Me in the day of trouble; I shall rescue you, and you will honor Me" (Psalm 50:15). We pray, God showers us with good things, and we honor him with thanksgiving and praise for his blessings. Where is the loser here? God has not lost anything, for his energy and power are endless and infinite. He will pour out blessings upon us forever and his glass will always remain just as full as it was at the start. Our problem is never that we ask for too much, or burden him too often, but rather we ask for too little, too infrequently, and often with evil motives (cf. James 4:3).

Prayer is simultaneously God-honoring and self-benefiting. Prayer is how we tap into God's sufficiency and comprehensive joy. "Ask and you will receive, so that your joy may be made full" (John

---

108 Piper, Desiring, 98.
109 Piper, Desiring, 182.

16:24). Prayer is an act of humility by which we honor God by asking God to bless us—to fulfill our needs and desires. Prayer benefits us in every way, and yet God, in his rich generosity, nevertheless gives us a heavenly reward for our prayers (Matthew 6:6). Fasting is, likewise, a personal, spiritual benefit to us for which God gives us an eternal reward (cf. Isaiah 58:6-11, Matthew 6:18).

In the same way, when God seeks honor and glory for himself through our worship, God is simultaneously seeking our highest pleasure:

> If my satisfaction in Him is incomplete until expressed in praise of Him for satisfying me, then God's effort to solicit my worship is both the most loving thing He could possibly do for me and the most glorifying thing He could possibly do for Himself. For in my gladness in Him is His glory in me.[110]

The old man seeks sin as his chief end and as a result of this he must forever feel that the world is a drab, frustrating place that stands opposed to his pleasure. His philosophy is a philosophy of death and adversity. The new man, on the other hand, knows that God has a plan and that behind even the most senseless suffering lies a good and perfect purpose. He looks beyond the world of sight and sees the invisible, spiritual reality that this world is perfect with respect to the end for which God made it: the ultimate glory of God and his children.

As the new man begins to define his glory in terms of God's glory, he begins to feel as if every molecule of this world is on his team, like so many loving fathers on the sideline, living vicariously through him and cheering for his absolute victory.

---

[110] Ibid, 218.

Why God Loves Christians
as Himself

A nts sometimes invade my kitchen in the fall, when the weather begins to get cold outside in Northeastern Ohio. I promptly use every means at my disposal to annihilate them. To tell you the truth, I do feel a little bit bad about it sometimes. I can't really fault the little buggers for seeking food and warmth and trying to extend their own little self-interested ant lives to the fullest extent possible. Still, their self-interest conflicts with mine. Whatever misgivings I might have about it, it's not enough to ever make me seriously consider relenting from the indiscriminate slaughter. I just can't be bothered with ants in the cereal boxes and other places I feel ants do not belong. I'm not particularly wealthy by American standards, but I suppose it speaks to my wealth, relatively speaking, that I feel compelled to throw out the whole box of cereal if I spot even one little ant in there. I just can't help but imagine the little soldier ants turning one of the cheerios into a makeshift latrine.

I'm sure they're quite wonderful creatures. I'm sure their endless industry is a tremendous blessing upon Ohio's ecology and all that. Yet, ultimately, the value I place on the life of an ant is clearly quite low at a practical level. I feel that a minor inconvenience to myself outweighs the value of hundreds of little ant lives, for I deem myself of much greater importance than them. By my reckoning, an ant is worth a little something and I am worth much more than him, but since he is finite and I am finite, the distance between our relative worth or value is a finite distance.

The distance between my worth and God's worth, on the other hand, is an infinite distance. If I am to be honest, that bothers me a little, for it follows, of course, that the value of a gross little ant and the value of a man are much closer together than the value of a man and the value of God. If an ant is inconsequential to me—smashed without a second thought—how much more so must I be inconsequential to God, with a never-ending chasm separating my glory from his glory, my significance from his significance? The ant brings a small ecological benefit to me by helping to sustain the local environment, but what benefit could I possibly bring to God, who literally existed in perfect contentment and absolute independence forever before I ever existed? King David asked the question very succinctly, but offered no answer:

> When I consider Your heavens, the work of Your fingers,
> The moon and the stars, which You have ordained;
> What is man that You take thought of him,
> And the son of man that You care for him?
>
> *(Psalm 8:3-4)*

The prophet Isaiah offered something of an answer, but you aren't likely to care much for it, and even less likely to find it in a Hallmark™ card anytime soon:

> Behold, the nations are like a drop from a bucket,
> And are regarded as a speck of dust on the scales;
> Behold, He lifts up the islands like fine dust.
> Even Lebanon is not enough to burn,
> Nor its beasts enough for a burnt offering.
> All the nations are as nothing before Him,
> They are regarded by Him as less than nothing and meaningless.
>
> *(Isaiah 40:15-17)*

It's not easy to hear that we offer nothing to God and are of no consequence to him, but "sure it is that, much as we have need of God, so much the more has God no need of us."[111] We add nothing to his being and "we have nothing of value that is not already His by right."[112] I don't know about you, but my inclination upon hearing this news is to throw my hands up in frustration and ask, *why bother with any of this then?* Whether misery or glory, one sort of self-interest or another, what difference does any of it make ultimately? If God accounts me meaningless, then presumably I should think God's thoughts after him and grant that I *am* meaningless. How can God rationally value that which, relative to himself, has no value? It stinks of irrationality and contradiction to say that "Jesus loves me" and that I am accounted by him "as less than nothing and meaningless."

That God should concern himself with us at all seems quite puzzling on these grounds. We should be surprised if we held his attention even for a moment. How strange then—how mysterious!—that God not only acknowledges our existence but pursues us even to the point of anger, jealousy, and personal anguish![113] The impression I am left with when reading my Bible is very much in accord with the impression left upon Lorenzo Valla six centuries ago:

> Every time that I hold in my hands the books called "canonical," in which is woven together the most sacred history from the beginning of the world, I recognize God's goodwill, care, and, I might say, solicitude toward us, so that he seems to me to have abandoned heaven in order to look after human affairs, [to] visit us, stay with us, admonish us, teach us in one place or another, and at length not to let

---

[111] Bolton, Bounds, 79%.

[112] Storms, Evermore, 60.

[113] On God's anger, see, for example, Romans 1:18, 2:5,5:9, 12:19. On his jealousy toward unfaithfulness, see, for example, Exodus 20:5 and 34:14.

us out of sight...unless some disgraceful crimes committed before his reverend countenance should force him to avert his face, and not only to avert his face but also (if it may be said) to break out in sighs and weeping. Yet he does not because of this desist from admonishing us; he calls, he reproves, he offers hope and fear, not like a schoolmaster, who [indifferently] accustoms children of whatever kind to letters by instructing, punishing, and encouraging them, but like a father, who has more concern for his own children. But why should I compare him to a father? We do not feel as great a solicitude for ourselves as he does. He cares for nothing else, he is never tired, he never sleeps, he watches over us while we sleep, he stands by us always, and never, finally, does he abandon us unless we repulse him, lifting our impious and ungrateful hands against him. O his incredible mercy and our obstinacy: a thousand times rejected and hooted off, yet he returns as soon as he is called, which not even our servants do—returns of his own accord, gentle, mild, gracious. As we fight against our salvation, he fights for it. May he win in this battle, he who has the power of conquest, and may we be conquered! Indeed, when he conquers us, we win, and when he loses, we lose.[114]

Still the question remains unanswered, however, why all this fuss over a few specs of dust? "What is man," asked Job, "that You magnify him, and that You are concerned about him?" (7:17). Why does God seem so intensely invested in us?

Perhaps the whole question is best relegated to the realm of the unknown? It is, after all, important to establish boundaries

---

[114] Valla, Pleasure, 285, 288.

between knowable and unknowable truths. What God has revealed to us is sufficient for our well-being, but God has not revealed everything to us. We know God has a visible form by which he chooses to reveal himself to us (Isaiah 6:1, Revelation 4, Revelation 18), but of his appearance we are given no meaningful description anywhere, and are accordingly commanded not to make an image of him, since that would necessarily entail vain speculation and, no doubt, some very unflattering guesses. We do not know when Jesus will return (cf. Matthew 24:36, Mark 13:32) or what exactly God has in store for us in heaven (cf. 1 Corinthians 2:9, 1 John 3:2), and, perhaps like these others, the question of man's significance is best relegated to the realm of the unknown.

Only an arrogant fool would propose to answer such a question as this in his own strength, yet I do believe that God, on account of his glory, has revealed the answer to us. Perhaps it was an overstatement to say David offered no answer to his question, for a closer look at the question may perhaps suggest that the question contained the answer. Maybe you noticed it. Perhaps it gave you pause. Why is it that God is mindful of the sons of men? Is it not on account of one of the sons of men? Is it not because of God's union with man in the person of the Son of Man? Is it not because, in the unity of that person, God is accounted man and man is accounted God, for that person is not only God, and not only man, but rather a God-man? Is it not because God foresaw his future communion with us, in Christ, that he valued us so richly even before the foundation of the world? (cf. Ephesians 1:3-6)

The Son of God seeks always to glorify God the Father because he is himself his Father's spitting image (cf. 2 Corinthians 4:4, Colossians 1:15, Philippians 2:6). Recognizing himself as one with the Father, as the Father's literal "other-I" you might say, he seeks the glory of the Father, because the Father's glory *is* his glory and, indeed, he *himself* is his Father's glory (cf. John 1:14). As the author of Hebrews put it, the Son "is the radiance of His glory and the exact representation of His nature" (Hebrews 1:3).

As the sun cannot exist without shedding abroad its glorious warmth and radiance, so too, the Father cannot exist without begetting his glorious Son.[115] Just as you could never have a sun without sunlight, or a fire without light and heat, so too you could never have a "Father" without a "Son" or a "Son" without a "Father," because the notion of a "fatherless son" or a "sonless father" is a contradiction in terms. The Father could not be a "Father" at all without his Son forever by his side. As the ancient Christian creed put it, "We believe in... the only-begotten Son of God, begotten of the Father before all worlds; God of God, Light of Light, Very God of Very God, begotten, not made, being of one substance with the Father."[116]

The Father, Son, and Holy Spirit, as perfect, infinite, mirror images of one another, perpetually echo and reflect one another's significance in a relationship of perfect love, harmony, and symmetry. The Father "has pleasure in his Son: he delights in the glory of his own perfections reflected back to him."[117] The Son of God is the infinite object of an infinite love, an infinite mirror perfectly echoing and reflecting an infinite glory. The circle of the Father's self-love naturally includes the Son and Holy Spirit, who are one with him. Each member of the Holy Trinity perpetually seeks to glorify one another, perceiving his own glory in the glory of the other, his own honor in the honor of the other, and, indeed, his own being in the being of the other. If the Father were to deny the Son, or the Son deny the Spirit, or the Spirit deny the Father, this would be to deny himself in the very same instant.

Since the Son of God is the "only begotten God" (John 1:18), begotten as light of light from the "Father of lights" (James 1:17), the Son saw it as entirely fitting that he carry the message of the Father's glory and warmth to the earth. He came on a mission

---

[115] See, for example, John Owen's helpful remarks in his commentary on Hebrews, chapter 1 and St. Augustine's unparalleled work *On the Trinity*.
[116] The Nicene Creed, as enlarged in 381 A.D.
[117] Piper, Pleasures, 157.

to glorify his Father (cf. John 17:4) by condescending to take on the form of a servant (cf. Philippians 2:7) in order to redeem mankind from sin (cf. John 3:16-17). "I have come as Light into the world, so that everyone who believes in Me will not remain in darkness" (John 12:46).

Though God is unchanging in his nature, as to who he is, a human man was brought into the divine fellowship by way of addition. The everlasting Son of God was united to a sinless infant around 5 B.C.[118] He was born in the city of David's birth, in a barn, in a town best known at the time as the place where sacrificial lambs were raised to be slaughtered in Jerusalem just a few miles to the north.

The Son of God came to unite himself to man, for he saw something to be gained for himself. He saw, in the first place, his Father's glory, and himself as the perfect reflection of it. "I glorified You on the earth," Jesus prayed, "having accomplished the work which You have given Me to do. Now, Father, glorify Me together with Yourself, with the glory which I had with You before the world was" (John 17:4-5). Jesus sought the Father's glory in all things so as to be glorified himself, as the radiance of his Father. He did not glorify himself immediately and directly but rather chose an indirect path. "If I glorify Myself, My glory is nothing; it is My Father who glorifies Me" (John 8:54). In glorifying the Father, he simultaneously glorifies himself as the Father's perfect reflection. "Therefore when [Judas] had gone out [to betray him], Jesus said, "Now is the Son of Man glorified, and God is glorified in Him; if God is glorified in Him, God will also glorify Him in Himself, and will glorify Him immediately" (John 13:31-32).

Accordingly, Jesus endured the cross "for the joy set before Him" (Hebrews 12:2), for he wanted "to purify *for Himself* a people for His own possession" (Titus 2:14). He knew he would soon be seated again at the right hand of the Father, having overcome every

---

[118] Jesus was born before Herod the Great died (since we know that Herod tried to kill him), and Herod died in 4 B.C. Thus Jesus was born no later than 4 B.C.

enemy and having gained a multitude of beloved brothers and sisters. Jesus viewed his sacrifice (the greatest of all conceivable sacrifices) not as a personal loss, but rather as the trading of a lesser value for a greater value. From his own divine perspective, he saw endless glory and praise following in the wake of a momentary suffering and humiliation.

It is a truth that sounds almost blasphemous when spoken aloud but a glorious truth nevertheless that in Christ *a man* becomes the proper object of human worship. I do not mean that he is *only* a man, but I certainly do mean that he is *truly* a man, as truly a man as ever there was, and yet truly the object of our worship. The two natures—the divine and the human—are always distinct, and never merged or confused, yet the unity of God and man in Christ is so perfect and, as it were, seamless, that the Bible freely attributes divine qualities to the human and human qualities to the divine. For example, in Luke 1:35, the angel said to the Virgin, the "holy Child shall be called the Son of God," though the Son of God, in his divine nature, was always The Ancient of Days and was never a child. Likewise, in Acts 20:28, it is "God" who "purchased [the church] with His own blood" though God, of course, does not have blood, for God is pure, invisible, immaterial, spirit (cf. John 4:24). Likewise, in John 1:14, the eternal Word "became flesh, and dwelt among us, and we saw His glory, glory as of the only begotten from the Father, full of grace and truth."

In the God-man, there is a unity in which God has blood as a man, and man's flesh shines with the glory of God. In the God-man, God's self-love and man's self-love, God's self-interest and man's self-interest are indistinguishably one and the same. Properly speaking, God did not become man, and man did not become God, but, rather, perfect deity was united to sinless humanity, and, on account of his perfect obedience, "God highly exalted Him, and bestowed on Him the name which is above every name" (Philippians 2:9), that is, the name of God.

The divine name was not bestowed upon the deity of Christ, for the Son of God always possessed the name of God by right; it was rather bestowed upon his humanity.[119] As the God-man, Christ Jesus of Nazareth is worthy of worship in his entire person, including his humanity. The English Puritan, John Owen (1616-1683), perhaps the greatest theologian of the modern era, rightly concluded:

> He who is the Mediator, or Jesus Christ the Mediator—is the object of all divine honour and worship. His person, and both his natures in that person, is so the object of religious worship.[120]

You could no sooner convince a Christian to stop adoring the body which was broken for them than you could get them to hate their own body. We worship the whole person; we can do no other.

My point in emphasizing the transcendent glory of Christ's *humanity* is this: I'm not sure how much a mere man can interest God, but a God-man is, no doubt, something God can get behind and be exceedingly passionate about. It is in Christ, therefore, that we must seek our highest and fullest significance. Indeed, here we begin to boast.

When Jesus overcame the world, defeated every enemy, and was drawn up into heaven as King exalted over all, he carried earth's exiles and outcasts with him in his train (cf. Psalm 68:18, Ephesians 4:8). It is only fitting that those with their hearts in heaven should celebrate with him and honor him in his victory in heaven. It is only fitting that those who were persecuted alongside him should also be exalted alongside him. Though his worldly audience imagined he was talking about setting up an earthly kingship, it was, no doubt, in prophetic reference to both his crucifixion and kingly ascension into heaven that Jesus said, "And I,

---

[119] See, for example, Matthew Henry's Commentary on Philippians 2:9.
[120] Owen, Glory, 119.

if I am lifted up from the earth, will draw all men to Myself" (John 12:32).

Christ's humanity is forever wed to his divinity, his divinity forever wed to the Trinity, and through our marriage union to Christ, God comes to love us as he loves Christ, which is to say, God comes to love us as he loves *himself.* Christians are wed to Christ, and Christ himself is the wedding, so to speak, of God and man, two natures in one person. Accordingly, the Father accounts those who are wed to Christ his beloved sons-and-daughters-in-law, his adopted children (cf. Galatians 4:5). We are accounted sons and daughters only on account of the Son. Had the Father not always a Son, neither could he have adopted us as sons and daughters.

God loved us on account of Christ even before the world was created. Even "before the foundation of the world" (Ephesians 1:4), God knew for certain what we would eventually be in union with Christ. He loved us "according to His kind intention which He purposed in [Christ] with a view to … the fullness of the times" (Ephesians 1:9). Just as God designed marriage to reflect our future covenant union with Christ, so too he sent his Son into the world to secure that perfect covenant union. "What did our Lord love in us?" asked Augustine. "He loved God in us! Not that we had God, but that we might have him."[121]

In the perfect communion of God and man in Christ, man finds perfect communion with God through him. He came from on high in order to draw us unto himself and to gain for us a higher significance. "For you know the grace of our Lord Jesus Christ, that though He was rich, yet for your sake He became poor, so that you through His poverty might become rich." (2 Corinthians 8:9).

God became a sacrificial servant to us to gain significance for us and a humble adoration from us significant creatures. In Christ, God leveraged his own significance to make us significant worshippers of himself, such that our value and significance, in his eyes, closely parallels his own. All men undoubtedly have a measure

---

[121] Augustine, On the Trinity, quoted in O'Donovan, Problem, 36.

of dignity and significance as created by God, as the children of Adam and Eve who were made in God's image, but the Christian has an astonishing degree of significance in Christ, for his head is placed in God's own family and a place setting established for him at God's own table (cf. John 14:3).

Every Christian can joyfully—marvelously!—proclaim, with David, you "have regarded me according to the standard of a man of high degree, O Lord God" (1 Chronicles 17:17). God purposed to make us significant in Christ, unto his own glory, even before the world was created (cf. Ephesians 1:4-5,11, 2 Timothy 1:9, Romans 8:29, 1 Corinthians 2:7). He set about the task of creation in view of the significance he himself would shortly achieve for us.

Apart from Christ, we could never do anything to earn a heavenly reward. I hope nothing I have said seemed to suggest the contrary. A man who fulfills God's commandments perfectly but tells just one little white lie (or, for that matter, fails to glorify God with his whole heart and strength for even a single instant) has broken the whole law (James 2:10) and must be punished as an offender. A slave who obeys his master perfectly has only done that which is expected of him, and it would be absurd for him to expect compensation (cf. Luke 17:10). "If you devoted every moment of your whole life exclusively to His service you could not give Him anything that was not in a sense His own already."[122]

It is only through Christ's death and our covenant hope in him that the corruption of our deeds is washed away and only on account of Christ's meritorious life that what remains is acceptable to God. It is only after we are established in Christ on the basis of faith that we can begin to speak meaningfully about laying up a heavenly reward. If you think you are good enough to merit a reward before God apart from Christ, you have gravely overestimated yourself:

---

[122] Lewis, Mere, 118.

Certainly, though we may do good works, and walk in the ways of obedience and with an eye to the recompense of the reward, yet none of us holds that these things are to be done with reference to our meriting of it.[123]

Another put it this way:

Certainly we do not say, nor is it our thought, that a person ultimately earns grace. O, what you learn first of all in relating yourself to God is precisely that you have no merit at all.[124]

Christ fulfilled the law in our place, took our punishment upon himself, earned us a right standing with God, and achieved for us a transcendent significance. "As the moon of herself can do nothing...if she does not receive light and heat from the sun, which is opposite her, so the actions of man were empty and worthy of punishment before they were illuminated by the light of truth and kindled by the heat of love, which is Christ."[125]

Our heavenly rewards are of grace, even as our redemption is of grace, even as our significance is of grace. "Oh, the awful emptiness of a full life when Christ stands yet without!"[126] Apart from first "putting on Christ" (Romans 13:4) like a coat of pure *importance,* you cannot expect to be rewarded like a son, but only like a criminal. To stand before God and not be put to shame, you must "adorn yourself with eminence and dignity, and clothe yourself with honor and majesty" (Job 40:10). To do that you have to forsake self-righteousness and seek the righteousness of God in Christ. "For all of you who were baptized into Christ have clothed yourselves with Christ" (Galatians 3:27).

---

[123] Bolton, Bounds, 69%.
[124] Kierkegaard, Love, 353.
[125] Valla, Pleasure, 269.
[126] Eliot, Shadow, 93.

Furthermore, it is God himself who brings about the desire to do good deeds in us through the Spirit of Christ. We cannot do anything apart from him (John 15:5). When God purposes to do us good, he gives us an assignment and then he gives us the will to start it, the strength to keep at it, and the resolve to finish it. And after he has done all the heavy lifting he rewards us for it, as though we did it all ourselves. He smiles upon us as an earthly father smiles upon the efforts of an eager but incapable toddler:

> When God has a purpose to give, He stirs up the heart to seek, and this stirring up of the heart to seek is an evidence that He has a purpose to bestow. He loves to bestow His mercy by way of [our] seeking [him], that we may be encouraged to come to Him, and to regard our blessings as the fruits of prayer and the performance by God of His promises to us. ...God gives both the grace of desiring, and the grace desired.[127]

Though created, in a sense, a little lower than the angels (Psalm 8:5), man is elevated high above the angels in honor in covenant union with Christ, so much so that we will sit in judgment over the angels (1 Corinthians 6:3). The angels themselves have the same difficult question about their significance, and I suspect the answer lies in the fact that they are servants of Christ and his brethren, the deacons of that true and final tabernacle. It is my personal opinion that the significance of every creature must inevitably, inexorably be traced back to Jesus Christ. He is the answer to every question and the prerequisite of every astonishing promise, "for as many as are the promises of God, in Him they are yes; therefore also through Him is our Amen to the glory of God through us" (2 Corinthians 1:20).

---

[127] Bolton, Bounds, 79%.

Reflecting God

The Son sits now with a glorified physical body at the right hand of the Father (Acts 7:55, Romans 8:34). He pleads our case before his Father (Romans 8:34) and he is able to sympathize with us in our weaknesses and trials, having been tested in everything and mistreated by men (Hebrews 4:15). And how can his intercession on our behalf not be successful when he appeals to his Father who is one with him? When he pleads our case based upon his own merit, can it be imagined the Father would turn a blind eye to justice? When the Father sent his Son on the mission to secure our redemption in the first place, can it be imagined the Father has no bias in our favor? Can it be imagined the Father would deny his Son and thereby deny his own glory and being? As if this were not already sufficient, the Holy Spirit also intercedes for us; the prayers we fail to pray, he cries out on our behalf (Romans 8:26-27).

Likewise, we ourselves "draw near with confidence to the throne of grace" (Hebrews 4:16), on account of Christ, as the adopted children of the Almighty, who, *legally considered*, are no longer capable of sin (cf. Romans 7:17, 1 John 3:9) because we've been fully justified through faith (Romans 3:28, 5:1). God has already proclaimed our innocence in Christ and nothing will change his mind. Sin still clings to us, like dust on our feet, but we ourselves are legally pure and spotless (cf. John 13:10-11).

Each day the Holy Spirit helps us to put to death the self-destructive desires of the old man by looking unto Christ (cf. Romans 8:13-14). As we look upon Christ, we become more like Christ. We even begin to see the glory of Christ as we look at ourselves in the mirror. "Now the Lord is the Spirit, and where the Spirit of the Lord is, there is liberty. But we all, with unveiled face, beholding as in a mirror the glory of the Lord, are being transformed into the same image from glory to glory, just as from the Lord, the Spirit." (2 Corinthians 3:17-18). The Holy Spirit works tirelessly to transform us—from glory to glory—into the image of Christ who is himself the image of his Father. Sinclair Furguson, the contemporary Scottish theologian, beautifully said:

> The purpose for which the Spirit is given is, therefore, nothing less than the reproduction of the image of God, that is transformation into the likeness of Christ who is himself the image of God. To receive the Spirit is to be inaugurated into the effects of this ongoing ministry."[128]

Though every Christian is already legally perfect, each of us knows we have a long way to go in practice. We know we are *justified* sinners just as surely as we know we are justified *sinners*. We know our sin alienates us from God in our day-to-day experience, as it is difficult to shout curses and to sing praises in the same breath. We long to be done with sin because we know it's nothing but a world of misery and self-defeat. Each day a Christian renews his mind through the working of the Holy Spirit in his heart (cf. Romans 12:2) and the regular means of sanctification such as Bible reading and prayer. Each day we get a little better at placing Christ before the eyes of our heart and becoming a little more like him (cf. Romans 8:29, Ephesians 4:24), a process which is ultimately and

---

[128] Ferguson, Spirit, 92.

immediately completed upon our final reunion with him (cf. 1 John 3:2).

In heaven, God will love what he sees in us, both legally and practically, without any reservations of any sort, because he will see himself reflected in us and live vicariously through us as his beautiful, spotless children. Likewise, we will love God because we will see in him everything good about ourselves, understanding, of course, that we have been conformed to his image and not the other way around. Having been renewed in his image, we will sing God's praises because we will see in him everything that is good and worthy of praise in ourselves.

We will also praise and honor and love ourselves correctly for the first time, seeing him in ourselves, just as we will praise and honor and love every other saint correctly, seeing all the same perfect qualities in them. Having all been conformed to that perfect image, we will never cease saying to one another "Well, aren't you fantastic!" and there will not be any insincerity in it; for the first time, we will actually mean what we say all the time. I am inclined to think, along with Valla, that everyone who bears Christ's image is famous in heaven:

> With what looks will they gaze upon you, with what voices answer your salutation, with what applause will they surround you, with what eagerness will they embrace you? You will swear that the eldest, as they throw their arms about your neck, are your parents, that those of your age are your brothers and sisters, that the younger ones are your children, or that they are all something yet dearer to you than parents, brothers and sisters, and children...[129]

---

[129] Valla, Pleasure, 311.

All of the Lord's illustrious brethren will praise and honor and love God with a singular heart and voice, hailing him as the original hedonist and the author and perfecter of all of our endless pleasure in him.

God could not deny the one who bears God's image and desires God's good without, at the same time, denying himself, which he cannot do. Nor could we ever deny the one whose image we bear and who desires our endless pleasure without at the same time hating our own flesh, but this we cannot do. "God, in seeking their glory and happiness, seeks himself: and in seeking himself...he seeks their glory and happiness."[130] As Piper noted, God, on account of Christ, seeks our good to the same extent he seeks his own good:

> With all His heart and with all His soul, God joins us in the pursuit of our everlasting joy because the consummation of that joy in Him redounds to the glory of His own infinite worth. All who cast themselves on God find that they are carried into endless joy by God's omnipotent commitment to His own glory."[131]

We will honor God with all our heart and with all our strength, seeing our honor in his honor and our significance in his significance. Astonishingly enough, God will do the same to us, since we are a reflection of him, reflecting his own glory back to him. As he has said, "I will rejoice over them to do them good and will faithfully plant them in this land *with all My heart and with all My soul*" (Jeremiah 32:41).

> For God, praise is the sweet echo of His own excellence in the hearts of His people. For us, praise

---

130 Edwards, End, 105.
131 Piper, Desiring, 54.

is the summit of satisfaction that comes from living in fellowship with God.

The stunning implication of this discovery is that all the omnipotent energy that drives the heart of God to pursue His own glory also drives Him to satisfy the hearts of those who seek their joy in Him."[132]

While sin will be banished and we will be perfectly conformed to Christ in moral perfection when we meet him, Edwards observed that there is also another important sense in which each child of God will become more and more like him in heaven. The quote is challenging, but well worth the effort:

> There are many reasons to think that what God has in view, in an increasing communication [or reflection] of himself [in us] through eternity, is an increasing knowledge of God, love to him, and joy in him. And it is to be considered, that the more those divine communications [or reflections] increase in the creature, the more it becomes one with God: for so much the more is it united to God in love, the heart is drawn nearer and nearer to God, and the union with him becomes more firm and close: and, at the same time, the creature becomes more and more conformed to God. The image is more and more perfect, and so the good that is in the creature comes forever nearer and nearer to an identity with that which is in God. In the view therefore of God, who has a comprehensive prospect of the increasing union and conformity through eternity, it must be an infinitely strict and perfect nearness, conformity, and oneness. For it

---

[132] Ibid, 53.

will forever come nearer and nearer to that strictness and perfection of union which there is between the Father and the Son. So that in the eyes of God, who perfectly sees the whole of it, in its infinite progress and increase, it must come to an eminent fulfilment of Christ's request, in John 17:21,23. "That they all may be one, as thou Father art in me, and I in thee, that they also may be one in us; I in them and thou in me, that they may be made perfect in one."…[In Christ, Christians are] brought home to him, united with him, centering most perfectly [on him, and], as it were, swallowed up in him: so that his respect to them finally coincides, and becomes one and the same, with respect to himself."[133]

Century after century, age after age, we will, in various ways, become more and more like our Father, for what could be more natural than for a child to honor his parent by imitation? As we come to think more and more of God's thoughts after him, our knowledge will be forever growing in approximation to his own infinite knowledge. Since God knows everything, he also knows what we will be like an infinite time from now, as an infinitely closer approximation of himself in that regard. At the same time that our knowledge of him is, little by little, ballooning unto infinity, we will be learning to love him more and more and our love for him will be inching ever closer to the matchless love shared between the Father, Son, and Holy Spirit. We will never actually arrive at the infinite, and must forever and always remain created, finite beings distinct from God. Nevertheless, we will always be diving deeper and deeper into the love and knowledge of God. The more we strive to plumb those endless depths, the deeper our love, pleasure, and

---

[133] Edwards, End, 101.

satisfaction in him will be. Though some glasses will be larger than others, every glass will grow perpetually.

To be sure, we will always remain distinct from God, but it is nevertheless true that through our union with Christ we come to possess a significance beyond that of created things. The Apostle Peter went so far as to say that, in Christ, we "become partakers of the divine nature, having escaped the corruption that is in the world" (2 Peter 1:4). The ancient church had a clearer sense of this scandal than the modern church. In the 4th Century, for example, Athanasius (c.296 - 373), the Bishop of Alexandria, asserted:

> For as the Lord, having assumed the body, became man, so we men are by the Logos deified, having been taken into partnership through his flesh, and, furthermore, we inherit eternal life.[134]

To be sure, it's not that we become God. Nevertheless, we mustn't lose sight of the profound significance of being transformed, through Christ, into God's offspring. C.S. Lewis is justified in speaking thus:

> He will make the feeblest and filthiest of us into a god or goddess, a dazzling, radiant, immortal creature, pulsating all through with such energy and joy and wisdom and love as we cannot now imagine, a bright stainless mirror which reflects back to God perfectly (though, of course, on a smaller scale) His own boundless power and delight and goodness.[135]

---

[134] Apologia Con Arianos, quoted in Seeberg, Doctrine, 212-213.

[135] Lewis, Mere, 163. Lewis seems to be referring to Psalm 82, where men are called "gods," a passage which Jesus used to defend his divinity. The expression, first used with reference to the Jewish people, is very thought provoking in this connection: "You are gods, and all of you are sons of the Most High" (6). When Jesus quotes the Psalmist in defense of his own divinity (cf. John 10:34), the context seems to imply that Jesus understood it to refer, in some sense, to all of

In Christ, God sees in us something worth fighting for, and—if it were possible—something worth dying for. Through the Son, God comes to value us as sons and daughters, the heirs of his infinite fortune (Romans 8:17).

Accordingly, we will praise him for the beauty of his disposition toward us, and he will praise us for the beauty of our disposition toward him. He will love us and we will love him, and we'll try to outdo him in love even as he will try to outdo us, and he will always be the victor in this contest, though we will win in his victory. We will honor him for his holiness and he will honor us for our holiness, for we too shall be perfectly holy. Whether it be love or praise or honor, every saint will echo and reflect it back and forth to one another in close communion together, and will echo and reflect it back and forth to God forever and ever. "You lose yourself in Him, to find yourself in Him when you are swallowed up in His likeness."[136]

We grow radiant as we look to him (Psalm 34:5). All the world tends unto the glory of God and we are the ones set ultimately on the path of reflecting his glory and, therefore, of glorying in his glory. Each day we will be more satisfied with him than the day before, even though we were perfectly and entirely satisfied with him the day before. We will, forever and always, seek his greater glorification, so that we may delight all the more in the warmth of those rays, to be warmed by it and to reflect it back to him yet again:

> The refulgence shines upon and into the creature, and is reflected back to the luminary. The beams of glory come from God, are something of God, and are refunded back again to their original. So that the

---

the children of God. The argument to the Pharisees seems to be, if the Bible says God has many children, why do you find it surprising that he has a Son?

[136] Bolton, Bounds, 89.

whole is of God, and in God, and to God; and he is the beginning, and the middle, and the end.[137]

In heaven, there will never again be a desire in your heart that doesn't find its fulfillment in reality, because our hearts will be in perfect conformity to God's heart, and whatever we ask he will give it to us, and we will praise him for it. In that place, "there will no longer be any night; and they will not have need of the light of a lamp nor the light of the sun, because the Lord God will illumine them; and they will reign forever and ever." (Revelation 22:5) Our faces will shine like the sun, as they reflect our Lord's face which shines brighter than the sun (cf. Revelation 21:23), and we who are the benefactors and recipients of his glory will forever seek to glorify him with all our heart, soul, and strength.

---

[137] Edwards, End, 120.

LOVE'S INFINITE DEBT

But when the Pharisees heard that Jesus had silenced the Sadducees, they gathered themselves together. One of them, a lawyer, asked Him a question, testing Him, "Teacher, which is the great commandment in the Law?" And He said to him, "'You shall love the Lord your God with all your heart, and with all your soul, and with all your mind.' This is the great and foremost commandment. The second is like it, 'You shall love your neighbor as yourself.' On these two commandments depend the whole Law and the Prophets."

(Matthew 22:34-40)

We normally think of love as a one-way street. To love someone else, in the most ordinary sense of the term, is to desire the best for them and to do what you can to support and sustain them. Love in this sense is outgoing, extroverted, benevolent, and sacrificial, heading out from us unto the benefit and blessing of our loved one.

This is only half the story of love, however. There is another dimension to love that is introverted, complacent, and self-interested. We noted this aspect of love at the very outset when we said true love always delights in its object. The love we feel for another, if it is sincere, is always a source of pleasure to ourselves. We enjoy our love for our beloved.

Just as we love our loved one in the extroverted sense, so too we love *our love* for them in the introverted sense, and these seem something like two sides of a single coin, which can be distinguished on paper, but never separated in practice. When we love someone, we seek to defend and protect them (in the extroverted sense) on account of the relation they bear to us and the pleasure they bring us (in the introverted sense). There is, in love, always a seamless union between self-love and other-love.

Take motherhood as a practical example of these two dimensions of love. Physically speaking, a mother gains very little from her child. A mother doesn't become smarter, wealthier, or more attractive on account of her child. In fact, carrying a child as a part of her own body for nine months requires sacrifice on a number of levels. I remember my wife browsing through pregnancy books when she was anticipating our first. She relayed how a woman's body pulls calcium out of her teeth and bones to supply her baby's ever-increasing calcium needs. I am inclined to accept it as true mostly because my wife's dental bills were astronomical a few years later. The child adds nothing to the mother's being, as such, and so a highly sacrificial, extroverted love is needed for the task. It seems that only a mother's love will do.

At the same time, every good mother attests that a mother discovers the greatest of rewards when she holds her child for the first time, namely, the reward of her own love for the child born in her image. "Whenever a woman is in labor she has pain, because her hour has come; but when she gives birth to the child, she no longer remembers the anguish because of the joy that a child has been born into the world" (John 16:21). The delight she takes in her love for her children repays her a thousand times over for the small physical sacrifices she has made. Under normal circumstances, it is the prospect of a future delight that made her desire a child in the first place. Her love for her child, even before that child was conceived, was built upon the foundation of her love for herself. She longed to see herself delighted with a child of her own.

It seems to me exquisitely beautiful in this connection that the inherently sacrificial act of nursing a child releases oxytocin and other hormones in the mother's body associated with happiness and well-being.[138] The mother is encouraged by nature (as designed by God) to nourish and delight in her baby unto their mutual satisfaction and well-being. Under normal circumstances, her own body literally signals to her that it is a pleasure to her to sacrifice of her body for her child. She learns something of sacrificial self-service in those early hours, and if she's paying attention, perhaps she also learns something of the delight God takes in his love for his children.

Before God created the world, an infinite number of ages elapsed in which there was nothing *but* God. God was alone forever before anything else existed. All through those endless ages, he loved himself as the highest thing to love and also as the only thing to love. The love begotten of his own nature turned happily upon itself, as he rested forever in peaceful stillness, joyous fellowship, and complete satisfaction with himself. God does not have to coerce himself to love himself perfectly like we do, but rather, it comes altogether naturally; he recognizes himself as the greatest conceivable being and he honors and glorifies himself accordingly, without the slightest reservation.

This love is singular, but also manifold. Just as the Father has an absolute moral obligation (to himself) to love himself as the greatest conceivable object, so too he has an absolute moral obligation to love his Son as the greatest conceivable object. "I and the Father," said Jesus, "are one" (John 10:30). The Father could not love the Son perfectly unless he loved himself perfectly, for the Son is his perfect reflection. God's introverted self-love is thus, at the same time, outgoing and extroverted. This law of Trinitarian self-love is no burden to God, but, rather, an infinite and unending delight, the endless echo of an infinite joy and love, exerted with endless energy and endlessly recycled into itself. The Father, Son,

---

138 Brown, Beyond, vii.

and Spirit love one another wholeheartedly, seeing their own good as identical with the good of the other, expending always an infinite energy in endless demonstrations of love to one another.

When the Apostle John wrote "God is love" (1 John 4:8,16), there can be no doubt that he at least meant that God's being is the foundation of all love, the heavenly pattern upon which all other love is necessarily founded. It seems as though our history is but a reflection of the divine history, something like God shouting his love for himself from the rooftops through us.

God redeems countless souls to mirror and reflect his own love back to him, as if to mightily affirm that though he has glorified his name forever, he has yet to grow weary of glorifying his name. When Jesus cried out "Father, glorify Your name.' Then a voice came out of heaven: 'I have both glorified it, and will glorify it again'" (John 12:28).

The Christian's great hope does not ultimately lie in the human will to love God forever, but, rather, in God's will to love and glorify God forever. A Christian is but the happy expression of God's love for himself. Our lives are a love story from God to God about God, in which we ourselves are remade in the likeness of God and shockingly—scandalously!—made the recipients of God's love for himself.

The Father has seated both his Son and the Christian on his own throne (cf. Revelation 3:21), as if to capture the weighty significance of his own reflection and all of the objects of his affection in a single glance:

> But God, being rich in mercy, because of His great love with which He loved us, even when we were dead in our transgressions, made us alive together with Christ (by grace you have been saved), and raised us up with Him, and seated us with Him in the heavenly places in Christ Jesus, so that in the ages to come He might show the surpassing riches of His grace in kindness toward us in Christ Jesus.
>
> *(Ephesians 2:4-7)*

Consider and imagine, oh Christian! The God who made all the pleasures and delights of this world with a mere breath has set you besides his beloved Son as a glorious bride, in order to demonstrate in you, through you, and upon you how much he loves himself reflected in the face of his children! The God of the universe has completely made up his mind. He has sworn by his own name (Hebrews 6:13) and, as it were, by his own blood, that, on account of Christ, he is going to do everything in his unlimited power to demonstrate in you the surpassing riches of his grace and love to himself! This world never conceived of such a heaven! Such a heaven could only be revealed from above. By thinking God's thoughts *after him*, we uncover the revelation of *God's heaven*.

To love God with all your strength is to love yourself with all your strength and to seek your own greatest happiness and pleasure. How extraordinarily great that greatest of all commandments to love the most *pleasurable* with all of our heart! Can we ever feel as though we have had enough of showering him with our love? No, "love never fails" (1 Corinthians 13:8), because love has the curious quality that the joy you feel as you pour your love out to another makes you feel as though something more is owed. Love is a gift to another that feels valuable to yourself.

When a young man falls in love with a young girl, we all know that his motivation for the flowers and chocolates and hand-written notes is not that he feels a disinterested sense of obligation to her, but, rather, that he feels grateful to her for the joy of his love. He feels he must repay her for his love by showering her with gifts. Love so enjoys its love and so delights in its love that it feels gratefully indebted to its object. Kierkegaard thought that giving away your love was something like coming into debt:

> When a man is gripped by love, he feels that this is like being in infinite debt... We shall not, then, speak about *one's coming into debt by receiving love.* No, it is the one who loves who is in debt; because he is aware of being gripped by love, he perceives this as being in infinite debt. Remarkable! To give a person one's love is, as has been said, certainly the highest a human being can give—and *yet, precisely when he gives his love and precisely by giving it he comes into infinite debt*...Usually we think the task is to get out of debt, whatever the debt is, a money debt, a debt of honor, a debt involving a promise—in short, whatever the debt is, the task is always rather to get out of debt, the sooner the better. But here it should be the task, therefore an honor, to be in debt!"[139]

He continues:

> Let us begin with a little thought-experiment. If a lover had done something for the beloved, something humanly speaking so extraordinary, lofty, and sacrificial that we men were obliged to say,

---

[139] Kierkegaard, Love, 172-173. His emphasis.

> "This is the utmost one human being can do for another"—this certainly would be beautiful and good. But suppose he added, "See, now I have paid my debt." Would not this be speaking unkindly, coldly, and harshly? Would it not be, if I may say it this way, an indecency which ought never to be heard, never in the good fellowship of true love? If, however, the lover did this noble and sacrificial thing and then added, "But I have one request—let me remain in debt": would not this be speaking in love?[140]

Though love forcefully expends itself for the good of the other, it does not, on that account, feel diminished, but rather kindled and intensified. Pouring our love into another does not make us love them less but love them more and feel all the more grateful for our love to them. Though love exerts itself toward the payment of the debt of love, the debt remains.

I always found it odd that Paul began so many of his letters by introducing himself as the *slave* of Jesus Christ (cf. Romans 1:1, Philippians 1:1, Titus 1:1), for no position in the world seems so undesirable as that of a slave. It sometimes seemed to me to be in poor taste to begin a letter of encouragement to other Christians with the dire prospect of slavery. I think we can make some sense of it, however, by recognizing that you typically became a slave in Paul's time when you couldn't pay your debt in any other way. You became the slave of your creditor until such time as your debt was repaid.

Paul undoubtedly saw himself as having an infinite debt to Christ, on account of Christ's sacrifice. Yet it must also be added that it would be contrary to everything Paul ever said—contrary to the whole spirit of the Bible really—to imagine that Paul felt as though he were in any sense the *unfortunate* slave of Christ. I do not

---

[140] Kierkegaard, Love, 173-174.

think this was the sort of debt he wanted to rid himself of, but rather the sort he wanted to keep, and to keep forever. "Having been freed from sin and enslaved to God, *you derive your benefit*, resulting in sanctification, and the outcome, eternal life" (Romans 6:22). Perhaps Paul thought of himself like the type of slave mentioned in Exodus 21:5, who, when asked if he wants to go out as a free man, immediately refuses. Without ever a second thought, he cries out, "'I love my master...I will not go out as a free man.'" God does not strike me as very humorous in the Bible (I suspect there will be plenty of that later on), but there is clearly no shortage of irony.

Oh, what glory! To be anchored forever to Christ in a world of love! I suppose we shall all have our turn reclining upon the Savior's chest at the supper table, like the disciple whom Jesus loved! (cf. John 13:23)[141] We will all say, with Solomon's bride, "Let his left hand be under my head and his right hand embrace me" (Song of Solomon 2:6).

Can we ever feel as if our debt of love has been repaid? No, let the debt be infinite, and let our slavery be an enduring slavery. To love God with all your strength is, at the same time, to pursue the highest conceivable pleasure for yourself.

So great is that greatest of all commandments, and the second is like unto it, for everything finds its proper place when God is the beginning and end of our love. How numerous the objects of love and, therefore, the sources of hedonistic pleasure the Lord has given us! When God is the beginning and end of our love, it becomes much easier to love your neighbor as yourself, for you understand that the man who loves everyone is the man who

---

[141] Whereas we sit upright and eat at the dinner table, the Roman world was a little smarter, and they would generally recline on the side or belly on a flat couch as they ate at a table level to them. Thus, Jesus was reclining while John rested on his chest as they ate the Passover together with the other Apostles on the eve of Jesus' death. This also helps explain what is meant by Jesus' curious expression "Abraham's bosom" (Luke 16:22) in reference to heaven. The image is of reclining upon Abraham's chest at the marriage supper of the Lamb.

enjoys everyone, and the man who loves most is the man who enjoys most.

If I am to love neighbor and parent and spouse and child and saint properly, I must also recognize that I myself am a neighbor, a parent, a spouse, a child, and—praise be to God!—a saint, and so I must also recognize myself as a proper object of love to the extent I am conformed to the image of Christ. Here on earth my self-love is highly imbalanced and unstable. I eat too much, for example, because I love my pleasure in eating, yet this is at my own long-term expense. In heaven, all will be a perfectly balanced, all-pervasive peace. Will I not love myself perfectly when I am perfectly conformed to Christ's image? To do otherwise would be an insult.

"Let all that you do," said Paul, "be done in love" (1 Corinthians 16:14). "Let no debt remain outstanding, except the continuing debt to love one another" (Romans 13:8 NIV) A Christian loves everyone on account of God and on account of himself being renewed in God's image. He sees God in himself and in everyone else. "The self that he loves is, as it were, enlarged and multiplied, so that in the very acts in which he loves himself, he loves others also."[142] Everywhere he looks he sees only children of God or potential children of God. "For to love God is to love oneself in truth; to help another human being to love God is to love another man; to be helped by another human being to love God is to be loved."[143] Oh Christian, let love be perfected in you:

> Beloved, let us love one another, for love is from God; and everyone who loves is born of God and knows God. The one who does not love does not know God, for God is love. By this the love of God was manifested in us, that God has sent His only begotten Son into the world so that we might live

---

[142] Edwards, Charity, 166.
[143] Kierkegaard, Love, 113.

through Him. In this is love, not that we loved God, but that He loved us and sent His Son to be the propitiation for our sins. Beloved, if God so loved us, we also ought to love one another. No one has seen God at any time; if we love one another, God abides in us, and His love is perfected in us. By this we know that we abide in Him and He in us, because He has given us of His Spirit. We have seen and testify that the Father has sent the Son to be the Savior of the world

(1 John 4:7-14).

Love is an infinite debt, and through Christ, we acquire an infinite energy to love. "The love of God has been poured out within our hearts through the Holy Spirit who was given to us" (Romans 5:5). In loving God, we reflect God's love back to God and thus channel God's infinite energy. We glorify him and are glorified by him in an endless cycle (cf. 2 Thessalonians 1:12). Like the widow's jar of oil, blessed by Elisha (cf. 2 Kings 4), after it is poured out completely it yet continues to pour out of a hidden, invisible, infinite reservoir. God makes us significant by his love and pours his love into us infinitely so that we may thereby glorify him in the most significant way possible, by pouring out our love to him forever.

There this glorious God is manifested, and shines forth, in full glory, in beams of love. And there this glorious fountain forever flows forth in streams, yea, in rivers of love and delight, and these rivers swell, as it were, to an ocean of love, in which the souls of the ransomed may bathe with the sweetest enjoyment, and their hearts, as it were, be deluged with love![144]

---

[144] Edwards, Charity, 328.

Heaven is the place where you discover the deepest satisfaction in perpetually pouring your love out to others, even as you are perpetually being filled by the love of others, all energized and empowered by the infinite, overflowing well of God's love.

The work of God in glorifying God will never end, and we must likewise always feel that there is more yet to pay on that blessed debt. Just as God has an infinite capacity and an endless desire to be glorified, so too we will have a corresponding endless desire to be forever satisfied by pursuing his glory. The always-unfinished nature of pursuing God's glory and expressing our love to God will forever be a source of exhilaration and unabashed laughter. After a hundred billion years, we will be glad to have finally gotten some of the formalities out of the way. The vision of God will not be the end of life, but merely the beginning. Jesus described heaven not as the end of life, but rather as *entering life* (cf. Matthew 18:9).

Christian love is always giving, yet never grows weary, always pouring itself out and yet always filled to the brim. It is always active, surging, boiling over, and yet always contented and at rest. Love always savors the present yet simultaneously longs for the future's hidden mysteries. Love never rests, never stops moving, never stops seeking to prove it is still alive and well within the chest. Love is always striving after a greater union with its beloved, always seeking to blur the line between the self and the other, always trying to pull the other into itself, as a second self, after the divine pattern. "What is love," asked Augustine, "except a certain life which couples or seeks to couple together some two things, namely, him that loves and that which is loved?"[145]

One question has perplexed me a great deal. Will we lose ourselves in God ultimately? Will we ultimately be swallowed up in him? The suggestion has been hinted at throughout all of Christian history. Will we be self-forgetful in the sense that we lose our

---

[145] On the Trinity, quoted in Sheldon, History, 214.

personal identity? I have considered it at some length, and I will give you my personal conclusion.

There is surely a self that will be lost. Away with the anxious self! Away with the fearful self! Away with the worried self! Away with this stressed out, worn out, heavy-laden, sick and tired self! Such a miserable creature has no place inside these blessed walls! This body of death will not survive the culmination of things (cf. Romans 7:24). The old man in us will surely be forgotten, gone forever, never to be seen again.

Nevertheless, as long as the Father, Son, and Spirit seek one another's satisfaction and honor and glory and praise, so too must the saint be present, as a *self* conformed to God's image and glory, to sing God's praises and to enjoy God with all of himself. There is a self that will be lost, but also a self which will endure. Even now the self-interest of the old man is fading away (cf. 1 John 2:17), but the self-interest of the new man stands upon the threshold of a complete glorification.

It is impossible—altogether unthinkable!—that Christian love should ever be a matter of indifference. Kierkegaard asked perceptively, "What would we think of a man who affirmed that he was in love and also that it was a matter of indifference to him?"[146] That impoverished Christian who has convinced himself that God must not be enjoyed has inadvertently doomed himself to be perpetually discontent with God and perpetually ineffective in the service of God. In the name of a false, worldly morality, he stamps out the flame of a warm and ardent love each time it reignites within the heart. He quenches the Spirit and steals a heartfelt, joyous worship from God at the same time he steals a heartfelt joy from himself. Love—true love—knows nothing of indifference, for love exults and delights in its love.

Though many people think we ruin good deeds by enjoying them, the Bible stands vehemently opposed to this. You will never be satisfied until you hunger and thirst for righteousness. You never

---

[146] Kierkegaard, Love, 43.

truly obey the law until you enjoy it. To love God's law is to walk in freedom (Psalm 119:45). Criminals hate the law, because the law opposes them, but a good man loves the law, for the law defends him from every sort of evil. God's law tells him where true pleasure is found. Heaven is the place where you never perceive legal restrictions or infringements upon your free will because your will is perfectly conformed to God's, and nothing gives you more pleasure than obeying God's good and perfect and pleasant law. Peace and rest follow all those who love God's law (Psalm 119:165). "Wherever the will conferred by the Creator is thus perfectly offered back in delighted and delighting obedience by the creature, there, most undoubtedly, is heaven."[147]

Some people suspect we might ruin God's worship by enjoying it too much, but the truth is, "God is not worshiped where He is not treasured and enjoyed."[148] It's always the case that "you honor what you delight in... [and] glorify what you enjoy."[149] Many people think you'll ruin obedience by delighting in obedience, but "certainly the more respect we have to the enjoyment of God in our obedience, the more noble is our obedience."[150] It is indeed unfortunate that "we all sin by needlessly disobeying the apostolic injunction to 'rejoice' as much as by anything else."[151]

The sin of indifference is so great in Christian culture today that it flouts itself openly as a virtue, as the most respectable of sins. So many times I have heard intelligent, well-educated Christians confidently say, "God doesn't command us to be happy," even though this is a tremendous, abominable lie! "Nothing can more properly be called love to any being or thing, than to place our happiness in it."[152] What a disgrace we offer to God when we refuse to be satisfied by him!

---

[147] Lewis, Pain, 602.
[148] Piper, Desiring, 22.
[149] Ibid, 307.
[150] Bolton, Bounds, 87%.
[151] Lewis, Pain, 587.
[152] Edwards, Charity, 165.

It is not enough to accept Christ out of a begrudging sense of duty and obligation, but rather you have a duty to "delight yourself in the Lord" (Psalm 37:4). You are commanded to "be glad in the Lord and rejoice, you righteous ones; And shout for joy, all you who are upright in heart." (Psalms 32:11) God has commanded us to "serve the Lord with gladness; come before Him with joyful singing" (Psalm 100:2). We must "rejoice in hope" (Romans 12:12) and "rejoice with those who rejoice." (Romans 12:15) We must "sing for joy" and "play skillfully with a shout of joy" (Psalm 33:1,3). Rejoice in his salvation, which is also your glorification (Psalm 21:1,5). And if you're still not sure what God's will for your life is, "Rejoice always; pray without ceasing; in everything give thanks; for this is God's will for you in Christ Jesus." (1 Thessalonians 5:16-18) Will you not rejoice in the God who rejoices in you?

> The Lord your God is in your midst,
> A victorious warrior.
> He will exult over you with joy,
> He will be quiet in His love,
> He will rejoice over you with shouts of joy.
>
> *(Zephaniah 3:17)*

"Rejoice in the Lord always" said Paul, and in case it wasn't clear the first time, "again I will say, rejoice!" (Philippians 4:4) There are over 800 such texts in the Bible.[153]

We have every rational cause for rejoicing, having come—by God's grace—to understand that God's good and our good align perfectly in our wholehearted pursuit of him. If a child insisted on being depressed and miserable, would this not also imply the depression and misery of their parent? To purposefully deny yourself Christian joy is to simultaneously deny God his rightful place on the throne. To purposefully deny yourself happiness in

---

[153] Alcorn, Happiness, 374.

God is to deny that God is cause for celebration. Why should you deprive yourself of this blessed contentment, when God has commanded it? Why will you insist on being miserable when the Lord has forbidden it? "Let the righteous be glad; let them exult before God; Yes, let them rejoice with gladness" (Psalm 68:3). When God demands your entire satisfaction in him and your complete contentment in all situations, why will you resist his will? When following the greatest commandment yields the best return for you personally, will you nevertheless insist on being impoverished? Is it not clear, friend, that in calling us to be Christians, God has called us to be hedonists?

If you've managed to make it this far, and yet it all feels too distant to strike you as personally relevant or meaningful, start by praying for your own satisfaction. Pray to God that God himself would be your greatest satisfaction, and that he would show you how to enjoy him more. God loves those sorts of prayers. An appeal to God to promote God's glory by being satisfied with God is a very compelling prayer to God. That's the sort of self-interest he wants from you. Pray that God would teach you how to obey him, how to be enslaved by him, how to rest in his all-sufficient, all-satisfying grace. Be relentless in praying to God that he would make you a happier Christian than you ever thought you could be.

The goal of the Christian life is a boundless pleasure in God through ceaseless worship and the major obstacle is sin, for sin makes God appear drab, just as God makes sin appear drab. Sin drags the heart out of heaven and into a hell of despair. The way to win the eternal wreath is to establish good, consistent, purposeful habits, to put God before your eyes as often and as purposefully as possible, so as to shift the trajectory of your life heavenward.

As you learn to faithfully obey God, you'll see that "the first reward of our obedience... [is] our increasing power to desire the ultimate reward."[154] As you obey more, you'll begin to hunger and thirst for righteousness. You'll discover a "holy happiness...that the

---

[154] Lewis, Weight, 14%.

more a man seeks and hopes for, the more he is quickened and enlivened in the disposition to be holy."[155] As good habits and obedience increase in your life, you'll discover an ever-greater delight in all the things of God. As you place your treasure in heaven through the practical exercise of your faith, you'll discover heaven growing in your heart.

As you fix your eyes on Christ, you'll find yourself becoming more and more like Christ, from one degree of glory to the next. As you become more like Christ, the more you'll happily place Christ squarely before you as the goal of all you do. The more you fix your eyes on Christ, the more you'll feel as though you've entered that blessed throne room early and the faster you'll run for that eternal prize:

> Therefore, since we have so great a cloud of witnesses surrounding us, let us also lay aside every encumbrance and the sin which so easily entangles us, and let us run with endurance the race that is set before us, fixing our eyes on Jesus, the author and perfecter of faith, who for the joy set before Him endured the cross, despising the shame, and has sat down at the right hand of the throne of God.
>
> *(Hebrews 12:1-2)*

Oh friend, I hope you run! I hope you run with all your might, and I hope you win.

---

[155] Edwards, Charity, 243.

BIBLIOGRAPHY

Adams, Jay. The Biblical View of Self-Esteem, Self-Love, Self-Image. Eugene, Oregon: Harvest House. 1995.

Alcorn, Randy. Happiness. Carol Stream, Illinois: Tyndale House Publishers, Inc. 2015.

Alcorn, Randy. The Law of Rewards. Wheaton, Illinois: Tyndale House Publishers, Inc. 2003.

Audi, Robert (editor). The Cambridge Dictionary of Philosophy. Cambridge, New York: Cambridge University Press. 1999.

Augustine of Hippo. On Christian Teaching. Oxford: Oxford University Press. 1997.

Axelrod, Robert. The Evolution of Cooperation. New York, New York: Basic Books. 2006.

Berkouwer, G.C. The Return of Christ. Grand Rapids, Michigan: William B. Eerdmans Publishing Company. 1972.

Bernard of Clairvaux. On Loving God. Kalamazoo, Michigan: Cistercian Publications. 1995.

Bloomfield, Paul (editor). Morality and Self-Interest. New York, New York: Oxford University Press. 2008.

Bolton, Samuel. The True Bounds of Christian Freedom. Unknown: Ravenio Books. Kindle Edition. 2013.

Brooks, Thomas. Heaven on Earth. Unknown: Monergism Books. Google Books. Unknown.

Bueno de Mesquita. The Predictioneer's Game: Using the Logic of Brazen Self-Interest to See and Shape the Future. New York, New York: Random House. 2009.

Burroughs, Jeremiah. Moses' Self-Denial. Unknown: Titus Books. Kindle edition. 2015.

Clark, Gordon. Thales to Dewey. Jefferson, Maryland: Trinity Foundation. 1995.

Copleston, Frederick. A History of Philosophy, Volume 1: Greece and Rome. New York, New York: Doubleday. 1993.

Dawkins, Richard. The Selfish Gene. Oxford: Oxford University Press. 1989.

Edwards, Jonathan. A Dissertation Concerning the End for Which God Created the World. The Works of Jonathan Edwards, Volume 1. Peabody, Massachusetts: Hendrickson Publishers. 2004.

Edwards, Jonathan. A Dissertation On the Nature of True Virtue. The Works of Jonathan Edwards, Volume 1. Peabody, Massachusetts: Hendrickson Publishers. 2004.

Edwards, Jonathan. Charity and Its Fruits. London, England: James Nisbet & Co. 1851.

Edwards, Jonathan. Christian Happiness (Sermon). http://edwards.yale.edu/archive?path=aHR0cDovL2Vkd2FyZHM ueWFsZS5lZHUvY2dpLWJpbi9uZXdwaGlsby9nZXRvYmplY3Q ucGw/Yy45OjQ6MS53amVVv

Edwards, Jonathan. The Life and Diary of David Brainerd. The Works of Jonathan Edwards, Volume 2. Peabody, Massachusetts: Hendrickson Publishers. 2004.

Edwards, Jonathan. The Portion of the Righteous (Sermon).The Works of Jonathan Edwards, Volume 2. Peabody, Massachusetts: Hendrickson Publishers. 2004.

Edwards, Jonathan. Safety, Fulness, and sweet Refreshment, to be found in Christ (Sermon). The Works of Jonathan Edwards, Volume 2. Peabody, Massachusetts: Hendrickson Publishers. 2004.

Epicurus. The Essential Epicurus. London, England: The Big Nest. 2014.

Elliot, Elisabeth. Shadow of the Almighty. New York, New York: Harper One. 1989.

Frankfurt, Harry G. The Reasons of Love. Princeton, New Jersey: Princeton University Press. 2004.

Fromm, Erich. The Art of Loving. New York, New York: Harper Collins. 2006.

Hills, Alison. The Beloved Self: Morality and the Challenge from Egoism. New York, New York: Oxford University Press. 2010.

Keddie, Gordon. Looking for the Good Life. Phillipsburg, New Jersey: Presbyterian and Reformed. 1991.

Keller, Tim. The Freedom of Self-Forgetfulness. Chorley, England: 10Publishing. 2012.

Lampe, Kurt. The Birth of Hedonism: The Cyrenaic Philosophers and Pleasure as a Way of Life. Princeton, NJ: Princeton University Press. 2015.

Lippitt, John. Kierkegaard and the Problem of Self-Love. Cambridge, UK: Cambridge University Press. 2013.

Lewis, C.S. Mere Christianity, The Complete C.S. Lewis Signature Classics. New York, New York: Harper One. 2002.

Lewis, C.S. The Screwtape Letters, The Complete C.S. Lewis Signature Classics. New York, New York: Harper One. 2002.

Lewis, C.S. The Problem of Pain, The Complete C.S. Lewis Signature Classics. New York, New York: Harper One. 2002.

Lewis, C.S. A Grief Observed, The Complete C.S. Lewis Signature Classics. New York, New York: Harper One. 2002.

Lewis, C.S. Reflections on the Psalms. New York, New York: Harper One. Kindle Edition. 2017.

Lewis, C.S. The Weight of Glory. New York, New York: Harper One. Kindle Edition. 2009.

Manton, Thomas. A Treatise of Self-Denial. Pensacola, Florida: Chapel Library. Kindle Edition. 2014.

MacIntyre, Alasdair. A Short History of Ethics. London, England. Routledge.1998.

Nygren, Anders. Agape and Eros. Philadelphia, Pennsylvania: Westminster Press. 1953.

O'Donovan, Oliver. The Problem of Self-Love in St. Augustine. Eugene, Oregon: Wipf & Stock Publishers. 2006.

Onfray, Michael. A Hedonist Manifesto: The Power to Exist. New York, New York: Columbia University Press. 2015.

Outka, Gene. Agape: An Ethical Analysis. London, England: Yale University Press. 1972.

Owen, John. Works, Volume 1: The Glory of Christ. Carlisle, Pennsylvania: Banner of Truth. 2000.

Piper, John. Desiring God: Meditations of a Christian Hedonist. Colorado Springs, Colorado: Multnomah. 2011.

Piper, John. The Pleasures of God. Sisters, Oregon: Multnomah. 2000.

Piper, John. God's Passion for His Glory: Living the Vision of Jonathan Edwards. Wheaton, Illinois: Crossway. 1998.

Rand, Ayn. The Virtue of Selfishness: A New Concept of Egoism. New York, New York: Signet. 1964.

Rogers, Kelly (editor). Self-Interest: An Anthology of Philosophical Perspectives. New York, New York: Routledge. 1997.

Schwartz, Peter. In Defense of Selfishness. New York, New York: Palgrave Macmillan. 2015.

Seeberg, Reinhold. History of Doctrines. Philadelphia, Pennsylvania: Lutheran Publications Society. 1905.

Sheldon, Henry C. History of Christian Doctrine, Volume 1. New York, New York: Harper & Brothers Publishers. 1895.

Storms, Sam. Pleasures Evermore: The Life-Changing Power of Enjoying God. Colorado Springs, Colorado: Navpress. 2000.

Vos, Geerhardus. Biblical Theology: Old and New Testaments. Carlisle, Pennsylvania: Banner of Truth Trust. 2004.

Watson, Thomas. The Duty of Self-Denial. Unknown: Unknown. Kindle Edition. 2010.

Weaver, Darlene Fozard. Self Love and Christian Ethics. Cambridge, United Kingdom: Cambridge University Press. 2002.

www.ingramcontent.com/pod-product-compliance
Lightning Source LLC
LaVergne TN
LVHW051055080426
835508LV00019B/1891